THE
TIME
OF THE
END

THE
TIME
OF THE
END

DON MANLEY

REDEMPTION
PRESS

Published by Redemption Press, PO Box 427, Enumclaw, WA 98022.
Toll Free (844) 2REDEEM (273-3336)

Redemption Press is honored to present this title in partnership with the author. The views expressed or implied in this work are those of the author. Redemption Press provides our imprint seal representing design excellence, creative content and high quality production.

Scripture verses are taken from the *King James Version* of the Bible.

Scripture quotations marked "NKJV" are taken from the *New King James Version*. Copyright © 1982 by Thomas Nelson, Inc. Used by permission. All rights reserved.

Scripture taken from the *New American Standard Bible,* © Copyright 1960, 1962, 1963, 1968, 1971, 1972, 1973, 1975, 1977 by The Lockman Foundation. Used by permission.

ISBN 13: 978-1-63232-380-4 (Print)
          978-1-63232-381-1 (ePub)
          978-1-63232-383-5 (Mobi)

Library of Congress Catalog Card Number: 2015939005

DEDICATION

This book is dedicated with great appreciation and gratitude to a very special couple: James and Elaine Young. They are members of the church I pastor and are wonderful friends who have helped me do the work God so graciously called me to do. They have encouraged me, prayed for me, and have been a great blessing to me. I love them, and thank God for them.

CONTENTS

Section III
The Prophetic Plan for Israel

ACKNOWLEDGMENTS

I want to thank my wife, Anne, for all of her help and for the encouragement she has given me. Without her kind words, faithful prayers, and great support, I could not have completed this task.

I also want to thank my office managers, Ann Evatt and Jackie DeMari, for their tremendous help in working on this project with me.

Then, there are my prayer partners. These are the people who pray for me, and my writing ministry, year in and year out. How grateful I am for their prayers.

Next, I want to thank the members of the First Baptist Church, Oxford, FL. Having heard me speak on the book of Daniel, they encouraged me to write this book.

Last, and best of all, I want to acknowledge my Savior, Jesus Christ. I thank Him, and I praise Him. I owe Him everything. He has brought joy, peace, and purpose to my life.

PREFACE

This book was written for you.

Are you a skeptic? Perhaps you are a seeker? Then again, maybe you are a believer? Some books that are written target a certain specific audience and the rest of us are excluded. Isn't that true? But that's not the case with this book. This book was written for you. Each of us fits into one of these categories. The skeptic says, "I don't believe." The seeker thinks, *I don't know what to think, but I sense that there is a God-shaped vacuum within me, and I find myself seeking answers.* The believer says, *"I have accepted Jesus Christ as my Savior, and I'm grateful that He saved me. But, I want to know more about the Bible; and yes, I want to know more about where our world is headed."* No matter what category you are in, this book was written for you. I had you in mind as I studied, prayed, researched, and wrote this book.

Why is there a Bible? God gave us the Bible because He loves us, and wants us to know Him. He is our Creator. He loves His creation. He wants to have a personal relationship with each of us. So great is His love for us. God, Himself, tells us in the Bible how we can have a personal relationship with Him. More on that later.

"Why is there prophecy in the Bible?" The God of heaven knows the future. In Old Testament times He often told His people about important events that would take place sometime in the future. Later, these events took place. God told His people of these events before they happened. That is prophecy. Prophecy is history written before it happens. Only God can do that.

One reason why God put prophecy in the Bible is to get our attention. He wants us to know that He, the God of the Bible, is *the* true God. Why is that important to God? Because He loves us. He wants you and me, and everybody, to have a personal relationship with Him.

There is another reason why God put prophecy in the Bible. He wants His people, the believers, to know what is going to happen in the future. Many view the Bible as an old, outdated book that is full of errors, but this thinking is wrong. Friend, your Bible is as up to date as tomorrow's newspaper! This will become evident to you as we study the book of Daniel.

Introduction
Daniel—The Key to
Understanding
End-Time Prophecies

Understanding the prophecies of the Bible is more important today than ever before. Events in our world are moving quickly. Many of these events point us right back to the end-time prophecies of the Bible.

The key to understanding the prophecies of the Bible, including the book of Revelation, is the book of Daniel. The famed theologian, Dr. John F. Walvoord, of Dallas Theological Seminary, said:

> In many respects, the book of Daniel is the most comprehensive prophetic revelation of the Old Testament, giving the only total view of world history from Babylon to the second advent of Christ and interrelating Gentile history and prophecy concerning Israel. Daniel provides the key to the overall interpretation of prophecy, is a major element in premillennialism, and is essential to the interpretation of the book of Revelation. Its revelation of the sovereignty and power of God has brought assurance to Jew and Gentile alike that God will fulfill His sovereign purposes in time and eternity.[1]

Two Important Questions

There are two important questions that need to be answered as we begin our study of Daniel. The first question is, "What is meant by the phrase 'the times of the Gentiles?'" The second question is, "What is meant by the phrase 'the time of the end?'" The answer to these two questions will prepare you for this study and will help you to more quickly understand the writings of Daniel. As you read this book keep your Bible close at hand.

Question #1—What is meant by the phrase "the times of the Gentiles?"

Christ used this phrase one day while sitting on the Mount of Olives with His disciples. Speaking to the disciples about future events (prophecy) He said. "Jerusalem shall be trodden down by the Gentiles until the times of the Gentiles be fulfilled" (Luke 21:24).

History tells us that the once proud, divinely blessed city of Jerusalem was "trodden down" by King Nebuchadnezzar of Babylon around 605 BC. You can read about that Babylonian invasion in 2 Chronicles 36:1-21.

Since Nebuchadnezzar's invasion (605 BC), Jerusalem has been "trodden down" by the Gentiles. When Christ sat and taught His disciples that day 2,000 years ago, who was the authority in Jerusalem? Well, it wasn't the Jews. It was the Gentiles. Rome. Let's fast-forward 2,000 years. Who controls Jerusalem today? It's not the Jews. Gentiles, namely the Middle East "quartet" of the United Nations, the United States, the European Union, and Russia make any major decision about Jerusalem today. Gentiles decide what the Jews can and cannot do in that troubled, divided city.

As we study the book of Daniel we will see that the city of Jerusalem will continue to be trampled on by the Gentiles until Jesus Christ returns from heaven and sets up His 1,000-year, worldwide kingdom. Guess where the capitol of Christ's kingdom will be? You guessed it— Jerusalem.

So the times of the Gentiles will not end until Jesus Christ returns. Who will be in control of Jerusalem then? Not Gentiles. Jesus Christ and the Jews!

INTRODUCTION

Summary:

"The times of the Gentiles" began with the Babylonian invasion of Jerusalem (605 BC) and will continue until the return of Jesus Christ.

Question #2—What is meant by the phrase, "the time of the end?"

There is a lot of interest today in the subject of "the time of the end." People everywhere are wondering, "What is happening to our country and our world?" It seems everything is in a state of crisis. There is turmoil and chaos at every turn. We see it in the governments of the world; we see it in our economic systems, in our institutions, and in our families.

There is a sense of gloom, of some unknown impending danger. There is the feeling that something is about to happen—but, what? Many people have given up watching the news or reading the newspaper. Some are saying things like, "I get depressed when I watch the news" or "I can't think about these things; it ruins my day," or "I wish I could just run away, but where would I go? There is no place to go." That is true. We simply cannot escape the problems of this world by a move from one location to another. Many have an ominous feeling that something big, something unknown is about to happen. Soon!

Is the "end" imminent? What is the meaning of that phrase in Daniel, "the time of the end?" That's a question that God wants to answer for you. The God of heaven is intensely personal! He loves each person as if that person were the only one to love. He gave us the Bible to tell us of His love. The Bible is a love letter written to you by someone who loves you a thousand times more that you and I can comprehend.

This personal, loving God wants you to know what is happening, why it's happening, and what is going to happen in the future.

The "Time of the End" is Not the End of Human History

The book of Revelation does deal with the end of time. That is why I entitled the book that I wrote on Revelation, *The End of Human*

History. The book of Daniel does not, however, deal with the end of this world. The "time of the end" in the book of Daniel is not the end of the world, it is the end of the age, referred to by Christ as "the times of the Gentiles."

The "time of the end" will last three-and-a-half years. It will end when Christ returns from heaven and sets up His kingdom here on earth (Dan. 7:25, 12:7; Rev. 13:5, 19:19-20). The "time of the end" is also called, "the time of Jacob's trouble" (Jer. 30:7) and "the great tribulation" (Matt. 24:21). It will be "a time of trouble, such as never was since there was a nation" (Dan. 12:1).

Cheer Up! Good News!

You could probably use some good news at this point, right? Here's the good news: if you have accepted, or will accept Christ as your Savior, before this soon-to-come "time of the end," you will escape all of the horrible trouble that is coming. Christ will take all believers out of the way before this awful time of trouble. One day soon He is going to appear in the sky, and call us up. We will rise to meet Him in the air! He will then take us safely to that place that He has prepared for us in heaven (John 14:1-6; 1 Thess. 4:13-17)! Then, the time of the end will come to the people left on earth.

Friend, I have majored on the prophecies of the Bible. If I knew what I know but did not have Christ as my Savior, I would be terrified at the things that are coming upon this earth.

The Great Stage of History

One of the most popular Bible teachers of the twentieth century was Theodore Epp. He was the featured speaker on the *Back To the Bible* broadcast. Here is what he said on our subject:

> We might compare the present time in world history to a great stage
> on which most of a play has already been acted out—only the last act

is yet to come. The curtain is still down, but behind it can be heard rumblings and movements as the stage props are being prepared for the last great, dramatic and climactic scene. The wars and rumors of wars, the peace talks and the plans for human survival are all part of the noises we hear, while at the same time the clouds of judgment are gathering. When will the last curtain rise? We are not sure, but Daniel takes us behind that curtain so that we need not be ignorant of what is coming. The world can only guess and wonder at what is taking place at the present time, and the best that anyone can do is plan for the present and the future. It is the privilege, however, of the Bible-believing student of prophecy to know what events are coming and what the outcome will be.[2]

Again, friend, God is intensely personal. He loves you. He wants you to love Him; and if you will, He will bless your life abundantly. He has told us in the Bible about major things that will happen so after these things happen, we will know that He is the true God. Why would He do that? Because He loves you.

The Ride of a Lifetime

In Disney World there is a roller coaster ride called "Space Mountain." People, especially kids, love it. Many have called it, "the ride of my life." As we are about to start our journey through the book of Daniel, a word of caution—hang on to your hat! This might be *the* spiritual ride of a lifetime!

SECTION I

THE HISTORY OF DANIEL THE PROPHET

Chapter One

THE SOVEREIGN GOD

Daniel 1:1-6

Do the things that happen to an individual, or to a family, or to a nation, happen just by chance? Is the God of heaven merely a spectator of this vast stadium called earth? Some would argue for the "God is a spectator" theory, but they would be in the minority. A large percentage of people would come up with an answer similar to this: "In some unknown way, God is working in our world. Just how He is working I do not know, but I truly believe that He is."

At the constitutional convention in Philadelphia in 1787, Benjamin Franklin stood and addressed the president of the convention, George Washington. He said, "I have lived sir, a long time, and the longer I live, the more convincing proofs I see of this truth—that God governs in the affairs of men."[3]

For the past forty-five years, I have studied the Bible seriously, and have also studied history. One thing that has been clear to me all through the years is this: the unseen hand of the almighty God has been active in the affairs of men from the very beginning and will continue to orchestrate the events of our world until time shall be no more.

In the final analysis, history is His story. The great pastor and Bible teacher Warren Wiersbe said:

> So wise and powerful is our God that He can permit men and women to make personal choices and still accomplish His purposes in the world. When He isn't permitted to rule, He will overrule, but His will shall ultimately be done and His name glorified. We worship and serve a Sovereign God who is never caught by surprise. No matter what our circumstances may be, we can always say with confidence, "Alleluia! . . . the Lord God Omnipotent reigns!"
>
> (Rev. 19:6 NKJV)[4]

The Invasion of Israel

> In the third year of the reign of Jehoiakim king of Judah came Nebuchadnezzar king of Babylon unto Jerusalem, and besieged it.
>
> (Dan. 1:1)

Jerusalem under attack? Jerusalem was God's special city, and these were His people! Why would God allow His city and His people to undergo an invasion by a pagan king?

The Reason for the Invasion

God allowed Jerusalem to be invaded because of the awful sins of His people, despite all the warnings that He had given them. God had His prophet, Jeremiah, warn them, but they would not listen. God also had His prophet Ezekiel warn them, but they refused to listen to him as well.

Warnings From Moses

Centuries earlier God told His people through His servant Moses, that they would be subject to discipline if they didn't live right. God said that if He disciplined them and yet they still failed to turn back to Him and correct their sinful ways, He would send another cycle of discipline, followed by a third cycle. If they still didn't repent, then He said there would be a fourth cycle of discipline, and finally a fifth cycle. These five cycles of discipline are outlined in Leviticus 26.

Hal Lindsey did an excellent job of breaking down these warnings from God to Moses. He referred to these warnings as "the doctrine of the five cycles of Divine discipline."[5]

The First Cycle of Discipline—Leviticus 26:14-17

In the first cycle of discipline there would be an increase of sickness and disease. Their economy would be disrupted by enemies. Their military would be involved in some limited wars, and they would lose. They would begin to lose some of their sovereignty to foreign powers.

The Second Cycle of Discipline—Leviticus 26:18-20

In this cycle of discipline, the nation would experience a power drain. Other nations would become more powerful. Changing weather patterns would destroy their agriculture, and hurt their economy. That would cause poverty, and shortage of food.

The Third Cycle of Discipline—Leviticus 26:21-22

In this cycle, the calamities would multiply. God said great numbers of their children would be killed. God also said He would bring yet another hard blow on their economy.

A Pause For Consideration

Do you see any similarities to these cycles of discipline and what is happening in the United States? The nation Israel was the people of God in the Old Testament. They were blessed with the light of God's Word. When they lived right and let their light shine to the other nations as a testimony to God, He blessed them. When they turned away from

Him, He disciplined them. If they proceeded to disobey, He proceeded to the next cycle of discipline, and so on.

America has been a nation blessed of God. He has blessed America with the light of His Word. But, how is America doing today? Consider the following: we are declining as a power rapidly. We are losing our kids to drugs, alcohol, crime, and all kinds of violence. We are experiencing much disease, in spite of our advances in medicines. Every time we think that we are going to eradicate disease, some new ones pop up.

America has had some limited wars, and we are beginning to lose. Consider these: Korea, Vietnam, and Afghanistan.

Israel had experienced all these things before the time we read about in Daniel 1:1.

The Fourth Cycle of Discipline—Leviticus 26:23-26

In this cycle of discipline there is a breakdown of government and of the nation's borders. Foreigners invade. There is famine. Godless foreigners rule the nation.

The Fifth Cycle of Discipline—Leviticus 26:27-39

In this cycle there is famine so bad there is actually cannibalism—parents eating their own children. There is the destruction of the nation, including its cities, and its worship places.

The Intrusion of the Temple—Daniel 1:2

And the Lord gave Jehoiakim king of Judah into his hand, with part of the vessels of the house of God: which he carried into the land of Shinar to the house of his god; and he brought the vessels into the treasure house of his god.

In verse two we see the *intrusion* of the temple, the Old Testament house of God. Nebuchadnezzar took some of these special vessels made out of silver and gold and carried them back to Babylon, and put them into the house of his false god. The subject of these vessels taken from the house of God will come up again later in the book of Daniel.

Notice in this verse, these vessels from the true house of God were taken, "into the land of Shinar." Shinar is the place where the Tower of Babel was built (Gen. 11:1-9). This was the fountainhead where all false religion started and then spread all over the earth.

So the vessels from God's house went into the house of a false god. Do you think there might have been an unseen spiritual war in progress here?

The land of Shinar (Babylon) is located in modern day Iraq. The people of Iraq are apparently proud of their ancient tower, Babel, as it has even been illustrated on some of their currency. What god do the Iraqis worship today? The Muslim god, Allah. Just a moment prior to the jet planes crashing into our Twin Towers on September 11th, what god did those foreign Muslim terrorists call on? Allah!

I submit to you my friend, that there is an unseen spiritual battle going on in our world today. Here in America it is a battle for the soul of our beloved nation.

The Indoctrination of a Jewish Teenager

Before heading back to Babylon, the Chaldeans rounded up several thousand Jews to take with them as captives. Among these captives were four teenage boys.

And the king spake unto Ashpenaz the master of his eunuchs, that he should bring certain of the children of Israel, and of the king's seed, and of the princes; children in whom was no blemish, but well favoured, and skilful in all wisdom, and cunning in knowledge, and understanding science, and such as had ability in them to stand in the king's palace, and whom they might teach the learning and the tongue of the Chaldeans. And the king appointed them a daily provision of the king's meat, and of the wine which he drank: so nourishing them three years, that at the end thereof they might stand before the king.

Now among these were of the children of Judah, Daniel, Hananiah, Mishael, and Azariah.

(Dan. 1:3-6)

These four teenage boys would be brainwashed and reeducated. Every effort would be made to get them to forget their God, the God of Abraham, Isaac and Jacob, and to embrace the gods of the Chaldeans. God, however, was at work behind the scenes, as He always is. God had a plan for these young men. What a shock it must have been for those boys. They were simply plucked from their homes, their country, and everything they knew and loved, and then forced to travel 900 miles east to a strange place called Babylon. Their faith, no doubt, was challenged with all of these events. Reading between the lines, I can see that God was with them, and I am convinced that He let them know that they were not to fear what men might do to them.

God always has a plan for those who are willing to give Him their all, and that includes those in the uncertain days in which we live. God wants His children to follow Him, no matter what. The unseen hand of God has been active in the affairs of man from the beginning and will continue to be until time shall be no more. Aren't you glad you are on His side? I want to encourage you to pray this prayer, or something similar: "Lord, no matter what, if you will lead me, and stay by my side, I will follow You."

Maybe you don't really know God. Maybe He's been doing things in your life to get your attention. Why would He do that? Because He loves you and wants to have a relationship with you. I don't know your story, and each story is different. But I believe He has been trying to get your attention. Why not reach out to Him in faith today?

Questions for Group Discussion
or Personal Study Emphasis

1. What has the sovereign God been up to in your life recently?

2. What do you think God is up to—

   • In our country?

   • In our world?

3. Describe the changes that have taken place in our country since your childhood.

4. What do you think God expects from His people (Christians) during a time of national moral and spiritual decay?

5. In your opinion, what is the greatest danger that America faces today?

6. Make a list of some things that we should be doing for God.

Chapter Two

THE RIGHT PURPOSE ℰ⟋

Daniel 1:6-21

In every age and in every generation, God searches for individuals who will follow Him, obey Him, and serve Him passionately. This has been the case all through human history. God is continually seeking ordinary people who will follow Him. He is looking for the individual who can truly say, "Lord, I am yours. I will do whatever you want me to do." That is just the person God is looking for and the person God will use.

Although teenagers, Daniel and his friends had already made that decision. It was no accident that these four Jewish boys from Jerusalem ended up in Babylon during the captivity. God had planned it. He knew all about these young men, just like He knows all about you and me. God knew they loved Him, and He knew they would live for Him no matter what. He chose these young men because they had the right purpose in their hearts.

The Placing of Daniel and His Friends

Great change had come in the lives of these teenagers. Their residence had changed. Forced to leave Jerusalem, they were now in Babylon

(vv. 3-6). Their education majors had been changed. Instead of studying Jewish culture, Jewish history, and Jewish law, they were forced to study Chaldean history, law, *and* religion.

Their food was also changed. Placed before them were foods that they had never tasted (v. 5). Their language would also change. They would have to learn and speak the language of the Chaldeans (v. 4). Their names were also changed. Their real names honored God. Their new names would honor the false gods of the Chaldeans. This was part of the indoctrination process to convert them to the false gods of the Chaldeans.

> Now among these were of the children of Judah, Daniel, Hananiah, Mishael, and Azariah: unto whom the prince of the eunuchs gave names: for he gave unto Daniel the name of Belteshazzar; and to Hananiah, of Shadrach; and to Mishael, of Meshach; and to Azariah, of Abednego.
>
> (Dan. 1:6-7)

The Hebrew name Daniel means, "God is my judge." His name was changed to Belteshazzar, which means "protect his life," with the name of a Persian god "Bel" implied. Hananiah means "the Lord is gracious." His name was changed to Shadrack, which means "command of Aku" (the moon god). Mishael means "who is like God." He was given the name Meshach, which means "who is like Aku is?" Azariah means "the Lord is my help." His name was changed to Abednego, which means, "servant of Nebo." Nebo was the second-ranking god in the Babylonian pantheon of gods. The true God was erased from their names. Their new names elevated the false gods of pagan Babylon.

Changed. Everything in the lives of these teenagers had changed, with only one big exception: God! He never changes (Mal. 3:6). He was still with them, and they knew it.

The Proposal of Daniel and His Friends

In the next group of verses we will discover Daniel's purpose, then we will learn of Daniel's problem, and then we will marvel at Daniel's proposal.

Daniel's Purpose

But Daniel purposed in his heart that he would not defile himself with the portion of the king's meat, nor with the wine which he drank: therefore he requested of the prince of the eunuchs that he might not defile himself.

(Dan. 1:8)

Back in Jerusalem, godly parents had raised these Jewish teens. Their parents were not part of the apostasy that had settled over the land of Judah like a dark cloud. Their parents were a part of the faithful remnant that still existed. They taught their sons the Word of God in their homes (Prov. 22:6). These teenagers, although young in age, were fully dedicated to the God of heaven.

Daniel's Problem

But Daniel purposed in his heart that he would not defile himself with the portion of the king's meat, nor with the wine which he drank: therefore he requested of the prince of the eunuchs that he might not defile himself. Now God had brought Daniel into favour and tender love with the prince of the eunuchs. And the prince of the eunuchs said unto Daniel, I fear my lord the king, who hath appointed your meat and your drink: for why should he see your faces worse liking than the children which are of your sort? then shall ye make me endanger my head to the king.

(Dan. 1:8-10)

There was nothing wrong with the quality of the king's food. It was probably the best food in all of Babylon. But, the Jews were under the law that God gave to Moses. In order to please God, a Jew could only eat certain types of meat, and the meat had to be prepared in a special way. The blood, for example, must be drained from the meat (Lev. 11, 17:10-16). In addition, the king's food would first be offered to idols. The idols and the gods the Babylonians worshipped were false, of course, but wherever false religion is practiced, demons are at work. Demons are real. They deceive people. They promote religion, and they seduce people into doing evil things. Daniel and his friends wanted no part of these things.

Daniel's Proposal

> Then said Daniel to Melzar, whom the prince of the eunuchs had set over Daniel, Hananiah, Mishael, and Azariah, prove thy servants, I beseech thee, ten days; and let them give us pulse to eat, and water to drink. Then let our countenances be looked upon before thee, and the countenance of the children that eat of the portion of the king's meat: and as thou seest, deal with thy servants. So he consented to them in this matter, and proved them ten days. And at the end of ten days their countenances appeared fairer and fatter in flesh than all the children which did eat the portion of the king's meat. Thus Melzar took away the portion of their meat, and the wine that they should drink; and gave them pulse.
>
> (Dan. 1:11-16)

"Daniel's handling of this problem sets the spiritual tone for the entire book," said Walvoord.[6] Commenting on these verses Warren Wiersbe said:

> How can God's people resist the pressures that can "squeeze" them into conformity with the world? According to Romans 12:1-2, "conformers" are people whose lives are controlled by pressure from without, but "transformers" are people whose lives are controlled by power from within. Daniel and his three friends were transformers: instead of being changed, they did the changing! God used them to transform the minds of powerful rulers and to bring great glory to His name in a pagan land.[7]

Daniel was wise beyond his years wasn't he? He had respect for authority. He kept a positive attitude. He used suggestions rather than demands. He was bold and courageous, and at the same time was tactful. The Spirit of God produces these qualities in believer's lives when they are yielded to Him (see Gal. 5:22-23).

The Promotion of Daniel and His Friends

> As for these four children, God gave them knowledge and skill in all learning and wisdom: and Daniel had understanding in all visions and dreams.
>
> (Dan. 1:17)

These teenagers were on a three-year crash educational course. God saw their dedication and honored them. Their Chaldean teachers must have been amazed at their ability to learn. Notice the word "wisdom" in this verse. The Bible teaches that there are two kinds of wisdom: man's wisdom and God's wisdom. Our educational system teaches human wisdom, but when believers come to the house of God to worship, they should expect and they should receive some divine wisdom, wisdom from the One who sits on the throne of heaven, wisdom that is revealed in the sacred book that we call the Bible. Wiersbe said:

> The Lord gave Daniel a special gift of understanding visions and dreams. In the first half of this book, Daniel interpreted the visions and dreams of others, but in the last half, he received visions of his own from the Lord.[8]

After three years of schooling it was "final exam" time. The king himself gave them the exam.

> Now at the end of the days that the king had said he should bring them in, then the prince of the eunuchs brought them in before Nebuchadnezzar. And the king communed with them; and among them all was found none like Daniel, Hananiah, Mishael, and Azariah:

therefore stood they before the king. And in all matters of wisdom and understanding that the king inquired of them he found them ten times better than all the magicians and astrologers that were in all his realm. And Daniel continued even unto the first year of king Cyrus.

(Dan. 1:18-21)

"Magicians" were those who dealt with the occult. "Astrologers" studied the stars to see if they could determine what influence their movements had on events. These were all forbidden by the law God gave Moses (see Deut. 18:9-13).

These young men were a tremendous testimony to everyone who came in contact with them.

The Eyes of the Lord

In every generation and in every age God looks for people whom He can use. He looks for ordinary people who He can empower to do extraordinary things in His service.

For the eyes of the LORD run to and fro throughout the whole earth, to shew himself strong in the behalf of them whose heart is perfect toward him.

(2 Chron. 16:9a)

His eyes are looking, searching everywhere for a few who will purpose in their hearts to serve Him, and to follow Him, no matter what. His eyes are going to and fro throughout the whole earth seeking for those whose hearts are right, so He can use them. He looks in the cities, He looks in every town and hamlet. His eyes scan the countryside. He must have workers for His great cause, and He always finds some. And when He finds them, He fills them with His power—power to overcome the temptations of this world. Power to serve God. Power to accomplish things that will count for all eternity. What an honor it is to serve Him!

Questions For Group Discussion or Personal Study Emphasis

1. God is always looking for men and women who will love Him and serve Him. When He finds such a person, He calls that person into His service. Some are called to do service for Him in the local church, others are called to serve Him full time in some other way. Can you think of some examples of men and women whom God has called:

   a. In biblical history?

   b. In history outside of the Bible?

   c. In modern-day history?

2. Things in our lives change from time to time. Sometimes these changes are difficult for us. Our God, however, never changes. In view of this great truth, list three things that He will do for you if, and when, a difficult change comes into your life. God will:

   1. _____

   2. _____

   3. _____

3. Memorize Philippians 4:19.

4. What things impressed you about Daniel in this chapter?

5. Daniel was blessed with two kinds of wisdom. What are the two kinds of wisdom found in the Bible?

    1. Wisdom that comes from _____

    2. Wisdom that comes from _____

6. How can we grow in the wisdom of God?

    1. _____

    2. _____

    3. _____

SECTION II

THE PROPHETIC PLAN
FOR THE GENTILES

Chapter Three

Two Nightmares and One Night Vision

Daniel 2:1-30

Our world is in a mess. In every age the great and good God of heaven needs people that He can count on to represent Him in this very needy world. In order to be an effective representative of the Lord, one must be in good shape spiritually.

Throughout my junior and senior high school years I was a wrestler. The wrestling season officially began every year on the first of November. The first few weeks of practice every year were brutal. Our wrestling coach was determined to get us guys in shape as quickly as possible, so he pushed us hard. The intense practices paid off, however. When the time came to wrestle other schools, we were ready. We were in good "physical" shape.

There were some special parents in Old Testament times. These special parents taught their children the Holy Scriptures from a very young age. They taught them who God is, what God expected from them, and they taught them from the Scriptures how they should live. They had their children memorize large portions of Scripture. I believe godly parents such as those raised Daniel and his friends. The powerful, flawless Word of God had shaped their thinking. Far from their homes in Jerusalem, these teenagers were about to face some tremendous spiritual battles. However, they were ready, for they were in top "spiritual" condition.

Millions of people today are concerned about their physical condition. Millions more are concerned about their financial condition. Both of these are very important to all of us. In addition, however, those of us who know Christ ought to also be concerned about our spiritual condition. In order to be the men and women that God wants us to be, we must discipline ourselves to spend some time reading the Bible, at least briefly each day, and let the Scripture sink deeply into our hearts.

Nebuchadnezzar's Nightmare

King Nebuchadnezzar of Babylon was the most powerful man on earth, but he was very insecure and troubled. Narcissists always are, and Nebuchadnezzar was a narcissist. Sam Vaknin, a leading expert on narcissism defines it as follows:

> Pathological narcissism is a life-long pattern of traits and behaviors which signify infatuation and obsession with one's self to the exclusion of all others and the egotistic and ruthless pursuit of one's gratification, dominance and ambition. As distinct from healthy narcissism which we all possess, pathological narcissism is maladaptive, rigid, persisting, and causes significant distress, and functional impairment.[9]

The Holy Spirit has been called the "cameraman" of Scripture. He focuses on what He wants us to see. As chapter two of Daniel opens, the cameraman focuses on the king.

> And in the second year of the reign of Nebuchadnezzar, Nebuchadnezzar dreamed dreams, wherewith his spirit was troubled, and his sleep brake from him.
>
> (Dan. 2:1)

The king had a nightmare! He then quickly called in his advisors. He called in the magicians who dealt with the occult. He called in the astrologers who studied the stars. He called in the sorcerers who practiced witchcraft. He also called in the Chaldeans.

Chaldea was a territory in lower Mesopotamia, bordering on the Persian Gulf. It was the area around the Euphrates and the Tigris Rivers.

So this elite panel of advisors quickly dressed and rushed over to the king's palace. Nebuchadnezzar had summoned them to come, and that meant *now*!

> Then the king commanded to call the magicians, and the astrologers, and the sorcerers, and the Chaldeans, for to shew the king his dreams. So they came and stood before the king. And the king said unto them, I have dreamed a dream, and my spirit was troubled to know the dream. Then spake the Chaldeans to the king in Syriack, O king, live for ever: tell thy servants the dream, and we will shew the interpretation.
>
> (Dan. 2:2-4)

The Advisors' Nightmare

Now we come to the second "nightmare" in this text, the advisors' nightmare. When a narcissist is confronted, criticized, or simply can't get whatever it is he wants, do you know what he does? He goes into a rage. He rages and he rages and he rages some more. Narcissists often surprise themselves at how quickly, and how powerfully, and how effectively they can rage.

The advisors told the king "tell us the dream, and we'll tell you what it means." Then the king got upset. He was unreasonable, as narcissists often are; then, like an angry lion, he raged and raged!

> The king answered and said to the Chaldeans, The thing is gone from me: if ye will not make known unto me the dream, with the interpretation thereof, ye shall be cut in pieces, and your houses shall be made a dunghill. But if ye shew the dream, and the interpretation thereof, ye shall receive of me gifts and rewards and great honour:

therefore shew me the dream, and the interpretation thereof. They answered again and said, Let the king tell his servants the dream, and we will shew the interpretation of it. The king answered and said, I know of certainty that ye would gain the time, because ye see the thing is gone from me. But if ye will not make known unto me the dream, there is but one decree for you: for ye have prepared lying and corrupt words to speak before me, till the time be changed: therefore tell me the dream, and I shall know that ye can shew me the interpretation thereof. The Chaldeans answered before the king, and said, There is not a man upon the earth that can shew the king's matter: therefore there is no king, lord, nor ruler, that asked such things at any magician, or astrologer, or Chaldean. And it is a rare thing that the king requireth, and there is none other that can shew it before the king, except the gods, whose dwelling is not with flesh. For this cause the king was angry and very furious, and commanded to destroy all the wise men of Babylon.

(Dan. 2:5-12)

A jury of one—the king—sentenced to death all of the advisors. They were terrified. What a nightmare!

Daniel's Night Vision

The scene shifts in verse 13. Then beginning in verse 14 the "cameraman" of Scripture is focused on Daniel. Some of Daniel's outstanding attributes can be seen in this portion of scripture.

Daniel Requests Some Time

Notice Daniel's strong faith and his strong communication skills.

And the decree went forth that the wise men should be slain; and they sought Daniel and his fellows to be slain. Then Daniel answered with counsel and wisdom to Arioch the captain of the king's guard, which was gone forth to slay the wise men of Babylon: he answered and said to Arioch the king's captain, Why is the decree so hasty from the king? Then Arioch made the thing known to Daniel. Then Daniel went in, and desired of the king that he would give him time, and that he would shew the king the interpretation.

(Dan. 2:13-16)

Daniel Requests Prayer

Notice next that Daniel and his friends were strong in prayer.

Then Daniel went to his house, and made the thing known to Hananiah, Mishael, and Azariah, his companions: that they would desire mercies of the God of heaven concerning this secret; that Daniel and his fellows should not perish with the rest of the wise men of Babylon.

(Dan. 2:17-18)

Daniel Receives the Night Vision

Next we will see that Daniel was strong in his walk with God. Daniel was about to receive a vision from God. When the Bible was still being written, God would sometimes give a vision to a man who was strong in his walk with Him. When a man was given a vision, unlike a dream, he was not asleep but awake.

Then was the secret revealed unto Daniel in a night vision. Then Daniel blessed the God of heaven.

(Dan. 2:19)

Daniel Rejoices by Praising and Worshipping God

Daniel answered and said, Blessed be the name of God for ever and ever: for wisdom and might are his: and he changeth the times and the seasons: he removeth kings, and setteth up kings: he giveth wisdom unto the wise, and knowledge to them that know understanding: he revealeth the deep and secret things: he knoweth what is in the darkness, and the light dwelleth with him. I thank thee, and praise thee, O thou God of my fathers, who hast given me wisdom and might, and hast made known unto me now what we desired of thee: for thou hast now made known unto us the king's matter. (Dan. 2:20-23)

Daniel was also strong in the Word. His prayer reveals to us that he knew the Scriptures well.

Daniel Rescues the King's Advisors

Therefore Daniel went in unto Arioch, whom the king had ordained to destroy the wise men of Babylon: he went and said thus unto him; Destroy not the wise men of Babylon: bring me in before the king, and I will shew unto the king the interpretation.

(Dan. 2:24)

Daniel Returns to the Royal Palace

As Daniel stands before the king, he testifies to him of the true and living God. Notice how strong his testimony was.

Then Arioch brought in Daniel before the king in haste, and said thus unto him, I have found a man of the captives of Judah, that will make known unto the king the interpretation. The king answered and said to Daniel, whose name was Belteshazzar, Art thou able to make known unto me the dream which I have seen, and the interpretation thereof? Daniel answered in the presence of the king, and said, The secret which the king hath demanded cannot the wise men, the astrologers, the magicians, the soothsayers, shew unto the king; but there is a God in heaven that revealeth secrets, and maketh known to the king Nebuchadnezzar what shall be in the latter days. Thy dream, and the visions of thy head upon thy bed, are these.

(Dan. 2:25-28)

Daniel Reveals the King's Thoughts Prior to His Nightmare

As for thee, O king, thy thoughts came into thy mind upon thy bed, what should come to pass hereafter: and he that revealeth secrets maketh known to thee what shall come to pass. (Dan. 2:29)

Daniel Reminds the King the Interpretation is From God

Notice how strong Daniel was in humility.

But as for me, this secret is not revealed to me for any wisdom that I have more than any living, but for their sakes that shall make known the interpretation to the king, and that thou mightest know the thoughts of thy heart.

(Dan. 2:30)

Daniel had some incredible qualities. In our text we see this Jewish teenager standing in front of the most powerful man on earth. Nebuchadnezzar, a pagan king, is seen listening to Daniel as he tells him about his God. Let's review the attributes of Daniel that we discussed in these verses.

- He was strong in his faith (vv. 13-16).

- He was strong in his communication skills (vv. 13-16, 27).

- He was strong in prayer (vv.17-18).

- He was strong in his walk with God (v. 19).

- He was strong in the Word (v. 21).

- He was strong in his testimony (v. 28).

- He was strong in humility (v. 30).

The Word of God and Spiritual Conditioning

Daniel was in great shape spiritually, wasn't he? Back in Jerusalem his parents had given him good spiritual training. The most important factor in our spiritual training is the Word of God. When we discipline ourselves to read the Bible each day, we grow stronger. The apostle Peter said:

> As newborn babes, desire the sincere milk of the word that ye may grow thereby.
>
> (1 Peter 2:2)

What kind of shape are you in spiritually? If you are in good shape take a moment right now and thank God for the work He has done in your life to get you to that place. Then, reaffirm in your heart that decision you once made to become strong in the Lord.

If, on the other hand, you are not in good shape spiritually, why not decide today to *take action*! Resolve today to become strong in the Lord! The apostle Paul, writing to the church in Ephesus, said:

> Finally, my brethren, be strong in the Lord, and in the power of His might.
>
> (Eph. 6:10)

Questions For Discussion or Personal Study Emphasis

1. Why has the Holy Spirit been referred to as the "cameraman" of Scripture?

2. Can you think of some good examples of this in other places in the Bible?

3. List as many of the seven attributes of Daniel (vs. 1-30) that you can.

4. Compare and discuss the training that Daniel and his friends received in their homes to the training that the average child receives in our culture today.

5. Compare our lifestyle today with the lifestyle that Daniel and his friends had in Babylon 2,600 years ago. In which culture would it be easier to be faithful to the Lord?

6. Why?

7. How should our answers to the above questions affect how we will live our lives in the future?

Chapter Four

THE NATIONS, DESTINY, AND GOD

Daniel 2:31-49

The Bible teaches that God is all-powerful, sovereign, and holy. Thinking people often ask, "If God is all-powerful and holy, how come there is so much evil in the world?" Here is the answer to that question. Although God is all-powerful, sovereign, and holy, when He created man He gave him a free will.

Man can choose to do right and serve God, or he can ignore God, serve some false god, or reject the concept of a creator altogether. The human race, for the most part, is in rebellion against God and that is why there is so much evil in our world.

Free will, however, has limits. The all-powerful, sovereign God can change the destiny of a man, or a nation, anytime He wants to. It is the Lord who removes kings and sets up kings (Dan. 2:21). The God of heaven determines the course of events that leads to the rise and fall of nations. He holds the destiny of every nation in His hands.

The Revelation of Daniel (vv. 31-45)

1. Daniel Reveals the Dream

The Old Testament was written in Hebrew, with the exception of Daniel 2:4-7:28, which was written in Aramaic. This was the language that was spoken in the land of Nebuchadnezzar, and the language that would later become the official language of the whole western section of the Persian Empire.

We pick up the story again in verse 31. The king is anxious to know about his dream. Daniel then begins to reveal to the king the things that God had revealed to him about the dream. First, Daniel will reveal the dream itself, then he will reveal the *meaning* of the dream. He will then reveal the source of the dream, and finally, he will reveal the *purpose* of the dream.

> Thou, O king, sawest, and behold a great image. This great image, whose brightness was excellent, stood before thee; and the form thereof was terrible. This image's head was of fine gold, his breast and his arms of silver, his belly and his thighs of brass, his legs of iron, his feet part of iron and part of clay.
>
> (Dan. 2:31-33)

The various parts of this image represent great empires, including the last world empire, which is yet to come. That coming empire will be extremely wicked. Its leader will viciously oppose the people of God on this earth and the God of heaven Himself.

Next, let's look at the stone in verse 34. The stone represents Jesus Christ who, when He comes back to earth, will destroy the last world empire and will then set up His kingdom. Christ's kingdom shall last forever.

> Thou sawest till that a stone was cut out without hands, which smote the image upon his feet that were of iron and clay, and brake them to pieces. Then was the iron, the clay, the brass, the silver, and the gold, broken to pieces together, and became like the chaff of the summer

threshingfloors; and the wind carried them away, that no place was found for them: and the stone that smote the image became a great mountain, and filled the whole earth.

(Dan. 2:34-35)

2. Daniel Reveals the Meaning of the Dream

In the next group of verses Daniel reveals to the king the kingdoms that are represented by the various parts of the image. The head of gold represents Babylon with Nebuchadnezzar as its king. Daniel also revealed to the king that it was Daniel's God that gave him his kingdom.

Thou, O king, art a king of kings: for the God of heaven hath given thee a kingdom, power, and strength, and glory. And wheresoever the children of men dwell, the beasts of the field and the fowls of the heaven hath he given into thine hand, and hath made thee ruler over them all. Thou art this head of gold.

(Dan. 2:37-38)

In verse 39 we read of two succeeding kingdoms. We know from history what kingdoms these were. The breast and the arms of silver represent the empire of the Medes and Persians.

And after thee shall arise another kingdom inferior to thee, and another third kingdom of brass, which shall bear rule over all the earth.

(Dan. 2:39)

The third kingdom represented by the belly and thighs of bronze was the kingdom that succeeded the Medes and the Persians—Greece. Later in this book, Daniel identifies Greece by name (Dan. 8:21, 11:2). In those days, a kingdom that had no rivals was considered to be the ruling power over all of the earth.

The empire that followed Greece was Rome. The legions of Rome were noted for their powerful, ruthless aggression. They would crush any resistance with an iron heel.

In AD 364 Emperor Valentinian divided the kingdom into two geographical areas: east and west. The two legs of iron represent the two parts of the Roman Empire, east and west.

> And the fourth kingdom shall be strong as iron: forasmuch as iron breaketh in pieces and subdueth all things: and as iron that breaketh all these, shall it break in pieces and bruise.
>
> (Dan. 2:40)

The Roman Empire was never destroyed, it decayed and then it simply fell apart. The Bible teaches that this empire will be revived and live again. The revised Roman Empire will be the last world empire of man. This is the one that will hate God, and the people of God. This is the one Christ will destroy at His second coming.

> And whereas thou sawest the feet and toes, part of potters' clay, and part of iron, the kingdom shall be divided; but there shall be in it of the strength of the iron, forasmuch as thou sawest the iron mixed with miry clay. And as the toes of the feet were part of iron, and part of clay, so the kingdom shall be partly strong, and partly broken.
>
> (Dan. 2:41-42)

The Bible tells us that ten national leaders will give their power to the coming world leader. God calls him the "beast." We normally refer to him as the anti-Christ (Rev. 17:12-13). The ten kings are represented in the image by the ten toes.

> And whereas thou sawest iron mixed with miry clay, they shall mingle themselves with the seed of men: but they shall not cleave one to another, even as iron is not mixed with clay. And in the days of these kings shall the God of heaven set up a kingdom, which shall never be destroyed: and the kingdom shall not be left to other people, but it shall break in pieces and consume all these kingdoms, and it shall stand for ever.
>
> (Dan. 2:43-44)

Notice the word "kings" in verse 44. What kings are these? These are the ten kings that we mentioned that are represented by the ten toes. Christ will come and destroy that wicked power, and then He will set up His kingdom.

3. Daniel Reveals the Source of the Dream

Daniel then tells the king where his dream came from. He tells the king that the source of the dream is the true God, Daniel's God (Dan. 2:45). The king is amazed at what he is hearing and sits in stunned silence.

4. Daniel Reveals the Purpose of the Dream

Daniel then tells the king that God's purpose in giving him the dream was to show what nations would rise to empire status in the future. To whom was he showing this? God first showed Daniel, then Nebuchadnezzar, and whomever else was in that throne room that night. Many, many others in that culture would embrace Daniel's God as their God. This dream was a given for our benefit also. This is one of history's most famous dreams. People have been reading this story, and telling this story, and writing about this story for 2,600 years! All who hear this story are made to ponder on this fact: the God of heaven knows what is going to happen before it happens.

> Forasmuch as thou sawest that the stone was cut out of the mountain without hands, and that it brake in pieces the iron, the brass, the clay, the silver, and the gold; the great God hath made known to the king what shall come to pass hereafter: and the dream is certain, and the interpretation thereof sure.
>
> (Dan. 2:45)

The Realizations of Nebuchadnezzar—Verses 46-47

Read the story over again; as you do, notice that Daniel, when ushered into the presence of the king, began immediately to testify to him about the God of heaven (vv. 27-28). Later when Daniel had finished his revelations, once again he witnesses to this ruthless king about the God of heaven (vv. 44-45). By the time Daniel was finished, Nebuchadnezzar comes to realize that the gods of Babylon were inferior to the Hebrew God.

Nebuchadnezzar realizes that Daniel's God is a great God.

Then the king Nebuchadnezzar fell upon his face, and worshipped Daniel, and commanded that they should offer an oblation and sweet odours unto him. The king answered unto Daniel, and said, Of a truth it is, that your God is a God of gods, and a Lord of kings, and a revealer of secrets, seeing thou couldest reveal this secret.

(Dan. 2:46-47)

Nebuchadnezzar realizes that Daniel should be promoted and be given a place of authority.

Then the king made Daniel a great man, and gave him many great gifts, and made him ruler over the whole province of Babylon, and chief of the governors over all the wise men of Babylon. Then Daniel requested of the king, and he set Shadrach, Meshach, and Abednego, over the affairs of the province of Babylon: but Daniel sat in the gate of the king.

(Dan. 2:48-49)

Secular historians can correctly identify major turning points in a war. They have told us, for example, that in World War II if Germany had finished off Great Britain before invading Russia, the war would have had a different outcome. Historians tell us if we had not been able to break the Japanese code in the Pacific, that war would have had a different outcome also.

Do major turning points in history happen "just by chance"? Some would say, "Yes, just by chance." But those of us who know the Lord, and have studied the Holy Scriptures, know that ultimately it is God who decides who will win and who will lose. He can even change the minds of national leaders so they will make whatever decisions He wants, without even being aware of His intervention. "The king's heart is like channels of water in the hand of the LORD; he turns it wherever He wishes" (Prov. 21:1 NASB).

The destiny of nations is in the hands of Almighty God. He determines what He will do with a nation based upon the people in that nation. He blesses obedience, and He judges disobedience. The Scripture says, "Righteousness exalteth a nation, but sin is a reproach to any people" (Prov. 14:34).

God also holds the destiny of every individual in His hands. The disobedient do not receive the blessings of God. His blessings are reserved for the obedient.

Nebuchadnezzar promoted Daniel, right? Well, sort of. God was really the One who promoted Daniel. That is just the way it always works.

> For promotion cometh neither from the east, nor from the west, nor from the south. But God is the judge: he putteth down one, and setteth up another.
>
> (Ps. 75:6-7)

If you are obeying the Lord in word, thought and deed, He is currently blessing your life. Many believers are not obeying the Lord. They are, therefore, not being blessed spiritually, and they are not happy. Children of the God of heaven are never satisfied with the "junk" of this world. If you are a believer yet find yourself longing for joy, peace, and purpose in life, decide today to be obedient to the Lord, and He will quickly add these things to your life. Here's a simple prayer for you to pray: "Lord, I am giving my free will back to you. I don't want it. I want your will. My destiny is in your hands, and now I am placing my will into your hands as well. Lord, you died for me on the cross; you paid for my sins, and now I will live for you."

Questions For Discussion
or Personal Study Emphasis

1. What is meant by "free will"?

2. Is God powerless in the affairs of man because of free will?

3. What determines the blessings of God upon a person, or a nation?

4. Is God blessing America?

5. Why did God give this nightmare to Nebuchadnezzar?

6. Who will destroy the last world ruling power? What will happen then?

THREE FALSE IMAGES

Daniel 3

Are you struggling with something in your life? If you are, you've got a lot of company. The bad news is Satan has filled the minds of men and women with wrong thinking of every kind. Wrong thinking always leads to problems. Man has searched for the answers to his problems for thousands of years but, try as he may, man cannot "fix" his problem of wrong thinking.

The good news is, God has the answer. The key to victory in one's life is the lordship of Christ. Regardless of one's weaknesses, fears, hang-ups, sins, or habits, the lordship of Christ is the key to victory. Lordship. What does that entail? Lordship means the person is no longer in control, the Lord is. Lordship only occurs when a believer turns his will completely over to the Lord. In essence, the believer says, "Lord, I'm yours, one hundred percent."

The Lord then, and only then, takes control. Suddenly, that believer now has power in his or her life. He can now battle the "demons" in his mind and win!

Nebuchadnezzar's False Image on the Plain of Dura

Several questions come to mind as one reads this chapter. We will attempt to cover five thought-provoking questions about this text.

Bible scholars believe the events of chapter three took place about twenty years after the events recorded in chapter two. With the passing of time, and the experiences of life, people tend to change. Nebuchadnezzar first invaded Jerusalem in 605 BC (Daniel 1), then, he invaded it again in 598 BC, slaughtering more Jews, and plundering the city. Finally, in 586 BC Nebuchadnezzar went back to Jerusalem, killed many Jews, destroyed the Jewish temple, and then burned the city.

The Image

In chapter two we see God humbling Nebuchadnezzar, but as chapter three opens, we see the king exalting himself. He thought he was the greatest man who ever lived, so he had an image built, which I believe was an image of himself.

In the dream that God gave him (chapter 2), there was also an image. The gold head represented Nebuchadnezzar's empire, Babylon. The king had twenty years to think about it. I think he probably came to the conclusion that, *I'm more than the head of gold, I'm the whole thing. My empire is going to last, well, maybe forever. I want an image just for me. I guess Daniel's God is not so great after all. I've ransacked that city three times, killed thousands of Jews, destroyed the city, and burned it.*

Question One

Our first question is, "Where is Daniel?" Daniel is nowhere to be found in this chapter. Daniel, remember, was promoted to a high government position. My guess is that he was out of the country on government business.

Nebuchadnezzar the king made an image of gold, whose height was threescore cubits, and the breadth thereof six cubits: he set it up in the plain of Dura, in the province of Babylon.

(Dan. 3:1)

The image probably had a frame of wood with beautiful overlay of gold. Notice the number six. The image was sixty cubits high and six cubits wide. The dimensions are puzzling. We don't know what the image looked like. It has been suggested that it might have been the image of a man standing on a pedestal.

Bible students read this and think about the image that men will be forced to worship in the last days, and its number 666 (Rev. 13:15-18).

When the image was completed the king sent out a decree to all the lands that he ruled. Representatives from all of these countries were ordered to come to Babylon for the dedication of the image.

Then Nebuchadnezzar the king sent to gather together the princes, the governors, and the captains, the judges, the treasurers, the counsellors, the sheriffs, and all the rulers of the provinces, to come to the dedication of the image which Nebuchadnezzar the king had set up. Then the princes, the governors, and captains, the judges, the treasurers, the counsellors, the sheriffs, and all the rulers of the provinces, were gathered together unto the dedication of the image that Nebuchadnezzar the king had set up; and they stood before the image that Nebuchadnezzar had set up. Then an herald cried aloud, To you it is commanded, O people, nations, and languages, that at what time ye hear the sound of the cornet, flute, harp, sackbut, psaltery, dulcimer, and all kinds of music, ye fall down and worship the golden image that Nebuchadnezzar the king hath set up: and whoso falleth not down and worshippeth shall the same hour be cast into the midst of a burning fiery furnace. Therefore at that time, when all the people heard the sound of the cornet, flute, harp, sackbut, psaltery, and all kinds of music, all the people, the nations, and the languages, fell down and worshipped the golden image that Nebuchadnezzar the king had set up.

(Dan. 3:2-7)

Why would the king want everybody to worship him? Simple. He was a narcissist and the narcissist loves praise and adoration. But wanting to be worshipped? Well, that's the ultimate high for the narcissist. Narcissists, you see, have to have attention, recognition, and the applause of men. They have to have it. It's like oxygen to them. The psychological name for this is called, "narcissistic supply." The king's image, however, was just one more false image.

Nebuchadnezzar's False Image of Himself—Verses 8-30

Let's discuss Nebuchadnezzar's other false image—the one in his mind. You wouldn't know it by the way they act, but narcissists are really insecure. Inwardly they feel inferior, unequipped, and thus, are insecure. A narcissist doesn't really like himself, so he hides behind a "mask." He plays a role. The image that he puts forth really fools people and he may even fool himself. He creates an image in his mind of his own greatness. He thinks he is always right. He becomes so taken up with this false image of himself that he actually believes he is special, he is deserving, and that he is in a league all of his own.

Narcissists are often found in places of authority. When they are, and someone under them fails to perform some duty, they will get very angry and rage. The narcissist will surprise himself during one of these outbursts of rage. He likes the fact that he can cause people to tremble and to submit to him.

The founder of the Chaldean dynasty of Babylon (or the neo-Babylonian dynasty) was Nabopolassar. When he died in 605 BC his son Nebuchadnezzar took the throne.

THREE FALSE IMAGES

Persecution

In this world, true believers are never far from persecution. The only thing that separates true believers from the onslaught of Satan is the hand of God. Daniel's three Jewish friends were about to go through a time of persecution.

> Wherefore at that time certain Chaldeans came near, and accused the Jews. They spake and said to the king Nebuchadnezzar, O king, live for ever. Thou, O king, hast made a decree, that every man that shall hear the sound of the cornet, flute, harp, sackbut, psaltery, and dulcimer, and all kinds of music, shall fall down and worship the golden image: and whoso falleth not down and worshippeth, that he should be cast into the midst of a burning fiery furnace. There are certain Jews whom thou hast set over the affairs of the province of Babylon, Shadrach, Meshach, and Abednego; these men, O king, have not regarded thee: they serve not thy gods, nor worship the golden image which thou hast set up.
>
> (Dan. 3:8-12)

When a narcissist is in a position of authority and yet he doesn't get his way, the result is predictable: rage.

> Then Nebuchadnezzar in his rage and fury commanded to bring Shadrach, Meshach, and Abednego. Then they brought these men before the king. Nebuchadnezzar spake and said unto them, Is it true, O Shadrach, Meshach, and Abednego, do not ye serve my gods, nor worship the golden image which I have set up? Now if ye be ready that at what time ye hear the sound of the cornet, flute, harp, sackbut, psaltery, and dulcimer, and all kinds of music, ye fall down and worship the image which I have made; well: but if ye worship not, ye shall be cast the same hour into the midst of a burning fiery furnace; and who is that God that shall deliver you out of my hands?
>
> (Dan. 3:13-15)

Decision Time

These believers in God had to make a decision: "Will we obey, or will we be killed? Will we bow, or will we burn?" That brings us to the next thought-provoking question.

Question Two

"What would I do if I'm ever in a similar position?" That question just automatically comes up in our minds as we read this text. I am not any braver than you, but if that day ever comes, and you and I have been living under His lordship, the question is settled. His strength will be there for us. Our Lord told the apostle Paul one day when he was praying, "My grace is sufficient for thee: for my strength is made perfect in weakness." Because the issue of lordship was settled in the apostle Paul's life he was able to say, "Most gladly therefore will I rather glory in my infirmities, that the power of Christ may rest upon me" (2 Cor. 12:9). He went on to say, "I take pleasure in . . . persecutions . . . for Christ's sake: for when I am weak, then am I strong" (2 Cor. 12:10).

> Shadrach, Meshach, and Abednego, answered and said to the king, O Nebuchadnezzar, we are not careful to answer thee in this matter. If it be so, our God whom we serve is able to deliver us from the burning fiery furnace, and he will deliver us out of thine hand, O king. But if not, be it known unto thee, O king, that we will not serve thy gods, nor worship the golden image which thou hast set up.
>
> (Dan. 3:16-18)

These Jewish believers answered the king humbly and respectfully, yet firmly. They would not compromise. Where did their great courage come from? Lordship. Any good psychologist could have predicted what would happen next. Rage! Anger!

> Then was Nebuchadnezzar full of fury, and the form of his visage was changed against Shadrach, Meshach, and Abednego: therefore he

spake, and commanded that they should heat the furnace one seven times more than it was wont to be heated. And he commanded the most mighty men that were in his army to bind Shadrach, Meshach, and Abednego, and to cast them into the burning fiery furnace. Then these men were bound in their coats, their hosen, and their hats, and their other garments, and were cast into the midst of the burning fiery furnace. Therefore because the king's commandment was urgent, and the furnace exceeding hot, the flame of the fire slew those men that took up Shadrach, Meshach, and Abednego. And these three men, Shadrach, Meshach, and Abednego, fell down bound into the midst of the burning fiery furnace.

(Dan. 3:19-23)

This text prompts our minds to ask another thought-provoking question.

Question Three

The third question is, "Where was God?" We will let the sacred text answer that question for us.

Then Nebuchadnezzar the king was astonied, and rose up in haste, and spake, and said unto his counsellors, Did not we cast three men bound into the midst of the fire? They answered and said unto the king, True, O king. He answered and said, Lo, I see four men loose, walking in the midst of the fire, and they have no hurt; and the form of the fourth is like the Son of God. Then Nebuchadnezzar came near to the mouth of the burning fiery furnace, and spake, and said, Shadrach, Meshach, and Abednego, ye servants of the most high God, come forth, and come hither. Then Shadrach, Meshach, and Abednego, came forth of the midst of the fire. And the princes, governors, and captains, and the king's counsellors, being gathered together, saw these men, upon whose bodies the fire had no power, nor was an hair of their head singed, neither were their coats changed, nor the smell of fire had passed on them. Then Nebuchadnezzar spake, and said, Blessed be the

God of Shadrach, Meshach, and Abednego, who hath sent his angel, and delivered his servants that trusted in him, and have changed the king's word, and yielded their bodies, that they might not serve nor worship any god, except their own God. Therefore I make a decree, That every people, nation, and language, which speak any thing amiss against the God of Shadrach, Meshach, and Abednego, shall be cut in pieces, and their houses shall be made a dunghill: because there is no other God that can deliver after this sort. Then the king promoted Shadrach, Meshach, and Abednego, in the province of Babylon.

(Dan. 3:24-30)

The Lord was there, wasn't He? This, we believe, was a pre-incarnate manifestation of Christ, or a "theophany." The Lord has not promised us protection from persecution, but He has promised us He will always be with us. Listen to His promise: "Lo, I am with you always, even unto the end of the world." (Matt. 28:20)

The Antichrist's False Image of the Tribulation

We have come to the end of the chapter, but there are still two thought-provoking questions that should be answered.

Question Four

The next question is, "Where is the prophecy in this chapter?"

Daniel is a book on prophecy. We have gone through the entire chapter and have discovered that the story in this chapter is historical. So where is the prophecy? Well, it is there, but it is in a different form. When we are reading a prophecy in Scripture, normally it's quite clear that it is a prophecy. Sometimes, however, the prophecy is in the form of a type. The events recorded in this chapter occurred nearly 2,600 years ago, but they serve as a type of the coming tribulation period.

The tribulation period occurs after the rapture of the church. All of us who are alive today who know Christ as our Savior will, because of death or because of the rapture (whichever comes first), be in heaven! Praise God we will not be here during the coming tribulation. Scripture tells us that an evil man will rise to world power. Satan will give this man his power, his throne, and great authority (Rev. 13). Bible students refer to him as the Antichrist, but God calls him "the beast."

Nebuchadnezzar in Daniel 3 is a type or a "picture" of the coming Antichrist. He will, by force, unite all religions into one. An image of the Antichrist will be made and the people of earth will be forced to worship that image. Failure to obey this command will result in death (Rev. 13:4, 7, 12, 15). The number six is associated with Nebuchadnezzar's image of the beast (Rev. 13:16-18). There is a close parallel between Daniel 3 and Revelation 13, even though the events of Daniel 3 occurred nearly 2,600 years ago, and the prophecies in Revelation 13 are still to come. Commenting on this parallel Lehman Strauss said:

> In both chapters there is a ruling despot and an image to be worshiped. Nebuchadnezzar is a type of the political "beast" who creates an image of himself as an object of state worship. In each instance the image is external, visible, magnificent, and impressive. The image in Daniel 3 is a type of an image to be erected by the Antichrist and set up in a Jewish temple. Our Lord refers to this image as "the abomination of desolation, spoken of by Daniel the prophet" (Matthew 24:15). Satan will perform a miracle by giving life to the image and causing it to speak (Revelation 13:15). Like Nebuchadnezzar's image, the image of the end time will be the object of wonder and veneration throughout the world. Daniel 3 is related to the beginning of the times of the Gentiles while Revelation 13 marks the end of the times of the Gentiles.[10]

During the tribulation the Jews will suffer a fiery persecution. The three Jews in Nebuchadnezzar's fiery furnace are a type of that coming persecution.

God's Answer for These Uncertain Times

These are uncertain times. People are worrying about the future. The hearts of many are filled with anxiety and fear. People are struggling with all kinds of earthly issues. Many believers in Christ are asking themselves, "Is there an answer; if so, what is it?" God does have an answer for us. The answer is the lordship of Christ. "What does that entail?" you might ask. The lordship of Christ begins in a believer's life the moment that a believer yields his or her will to the Lord. When the believer does that, the Lord lovingly fills that person's life with His presence. Soon after that, the fear, the worry, and the anxiety over the future are gone. Soon the confusion in the mind over earthly issues is also gone. Soon the sins that had enslaved that believer are also gone. In place of all of these, come new things into the believer—peace, joy and purpose for life. These are called "the fruit of the spirit" (Gal. 5:22-23). You can have all of this if you have accepted Christ as your Savior by letting Him be the Lord of your life. In these uncertain times, isn't this really what you want?

Question Five

Here is the final thought-provoking question: Will you let Christ rule in your life?

> I beseech you therefore, brethren, by the mercies of God, that ye present your bodies a living sacrifice, holy, acceptable unto God, which is your reasonable service. And be not conformed to this world: but be ye transformed by the renewing of your mind, that ye may prove what is that good, and acceptable, and perfect, will of God.
>
> (Rom. 12:1-2)

If you are willing to do this, here is the type of prayer you should pray: "Lord Jesus, here is my life, my will, my all. I invite you to take full control. Help me with my worries, my fears, my sins, and my weaknesses. Fill me, Lord, with Your love, Your joy, and Your peace. I am ready Lord, for You to give me a brand new life, and a brand new purpose.

Questions for Discussion or Personal Study Emphasis

1. How can a believer have the fruit of the Spirit in his or her life?

2. What is lordship?

3. How important is the lordship of Christ to believers during times of persecution?

4. List some ways that we as Christians are expected to compromise in order to fit in with everybody else.

5. Were the three Jews certain that God would deliver them? What was their attitude as they faced the king?

6. Who was the fourth person in the fiery furnace? How does this story apply to us?

7. A believer who is a narcissist can yield his or her life to the lordship of Christ. Discuss what the predictable results will be when a believer who struggles with narcissism yields his or her life to Christ's lordship.

Chapter Six

THE TESTIMONY OF NEBUCHADNEZZAR

Daniel 4

God created us to have fellowship with Him, but soon man sinned and that fellowship with the holy God was broken. However, the loving God of heaven was not about to give up on us. He would, instead, find a way to rescue us. He, Himself, would pay for our sin. Jesus Christ, the second member of the Godhead came to earth on a mission. He came to die on a Roman cross to pay for our sin. He would be buried, then He would rise again three days later. He promised to save from a burning hell all those who would accept Him as Savior by faith.

As I read the stories of the Bible, and as I talk to people today, I realize in every age God is at work in His world. He is always dealing with men, women, and youth about their need of Him. The God of heaven is loving, patient, and will go to great lengths to get a person to repent and accept Him.

Nebuchadnezzar Witnesses to the Pagan World—Verses 1-3

This chapter of Scripture is truly fascinating and abounds in unique qualities as it was written not in Hebrew, but in Aramaic, by Nebuchadnezzar, the king of Babylon. As Nebuchadnezzar speaks to us through the text we will see there has been a change in this man—a big change. The king has had a life changing experience with God. This chapter is a message from the most powerful man on earth to all of the people on earth. He wanted everybody to know that Daniel's God, the God of heaven, had changed his life.

> Nebuchadnezzar the king, unto all people, nations, and languages, that dwell in all the earth; Peace be multiplied unto you. I thought it good to shew the signs and wonders that the high God hath wrought toward me. How great are his signs! and how mighty are his wonders! his kingdom is an everlasting kingdom, and his dominion is from generation to generation.
>
> (Dan. 4:1-3)

What an amazing change there has been in the king's life. Instead of threats, he holds out the olive branch with the word "peace" (v. 1). Instead of insisting that people worship him, he points them to the "high God" (v. 2). Instead of praising his own kingdom, he praises God's kingdom (v. 3).

Nebuchadnezzar's Witness to the World—Verses 4-18

In the following verses we will learn that Nebuchadnezzar had another nightmare and was "troubled." A better translation would be "terrified." So, he called for all his pagan counselors. They all came quickly accept for Daniel. Where was Daniel? God didn't want Daniel there just yet. Then, after the counselors all failed to explain the meaning of the dream, Daniel was located and brought before the king.

God loved that wicked king. Isn't that amazing? God had placed four of His choicest servants into the king's life: Daniel, Shadrach, Meshach, and Abednego. Each of these men had witnessed to the king. Undoubtedly they prayed for his salvation year after year. The king was impressed and puzzled by something he saw in their lives he had never seen before: godliness. Then too, he had seen the power of their God. Daniel alone was able to tell the king about that first nightmare. He told the king the dream, and then he gave him the interpretation of the dream. Then the king watched in amazement as the three young Jews were brought out of the fiery furnace untouched by the fire. As one reads these early chapters in this book it becomes obvious that the all-powerful God of heaven was pursuing a relationship with Nebuchadnezzar the king.

I Nebuchadnezzar was at rest in mine house, and flourishing in my palace: I saw a dream which made me afraid, and the thoughts upon my bed and the visions of my head troubled me. Therefore made I a decree to bring in all the wise men of Babylon before me, that they might make known unto me the interpretation of the dream. Then came in the magicians, the astrologers, the Chaldeans, and the soothsayers: and I told the dream before them; but they did not make known unto me the interpretation thereof. But at the last Daniel came in before me, whose name was Belteshazzar, according to the name of my god, and in whom is the spirit of the holy gods: and before him I told the dream, saying, O Belteshazzar, master of the magicians, because I know that the spirit of the holy gods is in thee, and no secret troubleth thee, tell me the visions of my dream that I have seen, and the interpretation thereof. Thus were the visions of mine head in my bed; I saw, and behold a tree in the midst of the earth, and the height thereof was great. The tree grew, and was strong, and the height thereof reached unto heaven, and the sight thereof to the end of all the earth: the leaves thereof were fair, and the fruit thereof much, and in it was meat for all: the beasts of the field had shadow under it, and the fowls of the heaven dwelt in the boughs thereof, and all flesh was fed of it. I saw in the visions of my head upon my bed, and, behold, a watcher and an holy one came down from heaven; he cried aloud, and said thus, Hew down the tree, and cut off his branches, shake off his leaves, and scatter his fruit: let the beasts get away from under it, and the fowls from his branches: nevertheless leave the stump of his roots in the earth, even with a band of iron and brass, in the tender grass of the field; and let it be wet with the dew of heaven, and let his portion be with the beasts in the grass of the earth: let his heart be changed from man's, and let a beast's heart be given unto him; and let seven times pass over him. This matter is by the decree of the watchers, and the demand by the word of the holy ones: to the intent that the living may know that the most High ruleth in the kingdom of men, and giveth it to whomsoever he will, and setteth up over it the basest of men. This dream I king Nebuchadnezzar have seen. Now thou, O Belteshazzar, declare the interpretation thereof, forasmuch as all the wise men of my kingdom are not able to make known unto me the interpretation: but thou art able; for the spirit of the holy gods is in thee.

(Dan. 4:4-18)

Nebuchadnezzar's Testimony About a Servant of God— Verses 19-27

The "watcher" mentioned in our text (v. 13, 17, 23) is no doubt an angel. Daniel was given the interpretation of the dream and was appalled. God was going to give this powerful king the mind of a beast. For seven years he would live with the beasts of the field and would eat grass. The God of heaven would soon humble this proud king.

Some "know it all" narcissists must be greatly humbled before they will recognize their need for salvation. That was the case with Nebuchadnezzar. After Daniel gave the king the interpretation of the dream, he gave him some advice. He told him to stop sinning and to have mercy on the poor (which he apparently didn't have) and maybe God would prolong the inevitable.

Then Daniel, whose name was Belteshazzar, was astonied for one hour, and his thoughts troubled him. The king spake, and said, Belteshazzar, let not the dream, or the interpretation thereof, trouble thee. Belteshazzar answered and said, My lord, the dream be to them that hate thee, and the interpretation thereof to thine enemies. The tree that thou sawest, which grew, and was strong, whose height reached unto the heaven, and the sight thereof to all the earth; whose leaves were fair, and the fruit thereof much, and in it was meat for all; under which the beasts of the field dwelt, and upon whose branches

74

the fowls of the heaven had their habitation: it is thou, O king, that art grown and become strong: for thy greatness is grown, and reacheth unto heaven, and thy dominion to the end of the earth. And whereas the king saw a watcher and an holy one coming down from heaven, and saying, Hew the tree down, and destroy it; yet leave the stump of the roots thereof in the earth, even with a band of iron and brass, in the tender grass of the field; and let it be wet with the dew of heaven, and let his portion be with the beasts of the field, till seven times pass over him; this is the interpretation, O king, and this is the decree of the most High, which is come upon my lord the king: That they shall drive thee from men, and thy dwelling shall be with the beasts of the field, and they shall make thee to eat grass as oxen, and they shall wet thee with the dew of heaven, and seven times shall pass over thee, till thou know that the most High ruleth in the kingdom of men, and giveth it to whomsoever he will. And whereas they commanded to leave the stump of the tree roots; thy kingdom shall be sure unto thee, after that thou shalt have known that the heavens do rule. Wherefore, O king, let my counsel be acceptable unto thee, and break off thy sins by righteousness, and thine iniquities by shewing mercy to the poor; if it may be a lengthening of thy tranquility.

(Dan. 4:19-27)

Nebuchadnezzar's Humbling Experience at the Hand of Almighty God—Verses 28-36

A whole year went by and nothing happened. Then one day the king was in his palace. He was apparently walking around the flat roof of the palace, admiring the beautiful city of Babylon that he had built up. At the same time he was admiring himself and was full of pride. Pride is a destructive force. God hates pride (Prov. 6:16). "Pride goeth before destruction and an haughty spirit before a fall" (Prov. 16:18).

Nebuchadnezzar built up the city of Babylon as a monument to himself. While Nebuchadnezzar was bragging, God suddenly interrupted him and let him know his day had come.

All this came upon the king Nebuchadnezzar. At the end of twelve months he walked in the palace of the kingdom of Babylon. The king spake, and said, Is not this great Babylon, that I have built for the house of the kingdom by the might of my power, and for the honour of my majesty? While the word was in the king's mouth, there fell a voice from heaven, saying, O king Nebuchadnezzar, to thee it is spoken; The kingdom is departed from thee. And they shall drive thee from men, and thy dwelling shall be with the beasts of the field: they shall make thee to eat grass as oxen, and seven times shall pass over thee, until thou know that the most High ruleth in the kingdom of men, and giveth it to whomsoever he will. The same hour was the thing fulfilled upon Nebuchadnezzar: and he was driven from men, and did eat grass as oxen, and his body was wet with the dew of heaven, till his hairs were grown like eagles' feathers, and his nails like birds' claws.

(Dan. 4:28-33)

Have you ever heard of *boanthropy*? It is a rare form of insanity; a psychological disorder in which a human being believes himself to be an ox or a cow, and attempts to live accordingly. The insane person, however, still retains an inner consciousness. This seems to describe Nebuchadnezzar's God-induced illness.

And at the end of the days I Nebuchadnezzar lifted up mine eyes unto heaven, and mine understanding returned unto me, and I blessed the most High, and I praised and honoured him that liveth for ever, whose dominion is an everlasting dominion, and his kingdom is from generation to generation: and all the inhabitants of the earth are reputed as nothing: and he doeth according to his will in the army of heaven, and among the inhabitants of the earth: and none can stay his hand, or say unto him, What doest thou? At the same time my reason returned unto me; and for the glory of my kingdom, mine honour and brightness returned unto me; and my counsellors and my lords sought unto me; and I was established in my kingdom, and excellent majesty was added unto me. Now I Nebuchadnezzar praise and extol and honour the King of heaven, all whose works are truth, and his ways judgment: and those that walk in pride he is able to abase.

(Dan. 4:34-37)

Nebuchadnezzar Again Witnesses to the People of Earth

God had dealt with Nebuchadnezzar's pride, so now, instead of trying to elevate himself, he lifts up God. By doing that Nebuchadnezzar was witnessing to all of the people in his empire. Notice in verse 37 he speaks about the "King of heaven." His name is Jesus Christ. One day that king is going to come riding down in the clouds on a white horse. He'll have a name written on His robe. It will say, "King of Kings, and Lord of Lords" (Rev. 19:16).

Over 2,500 years ago God pursued a loving relationship with the wicked king of Babylon and He is still pursuing people today. He said, "For I, the Lord, do not change" (Mal. 3:6 NASB). Sometimes He will do something in our lives that is important in order to get our attention. Then, if we will listen, He will speak. God speaks to us today through conscience, through the lives and testimonies of believers who love Him, and through His written Word, the Bible. He sometimes gets a person's attention by placing a problem or a crisis in a person's life. He pursues the unsaved of our world because He is "not willing that any should perish, but that all should come to repentance" (2 Peter 3:9).

Some of God's people do not experience meaningful fellowship with Him because of sin and self will. God is pursuing them as well. He pursues us because He wants and desires fellowship with us.

Are you facing a problem? Is there an obstacle in your path? Is there a crisis? Trouble in our lives will make us *bitter* or *better*, depending upon what we do with it. Sometimes we are hardheaded and will not turn to God. Bitterness and confusion are the results. God pursues us during times of trouble. If we turn to Him, joy and peace will always result. "And we know that all things work together for good to them that love God, to them who are the called according to his purpose" (Rom. 8:28).

Questions for Discussion
or Personal Study Emphasis

1. Daniel and his three friends were taken from their homeland and, even though they loved the Lord, were made to live in Babylon. Why? Discuss possible reasons.

2. Memorize Romans 8:28.

3. Why do you think God hates pride?

4. God looked beyond Nebuchadnezzar's great sin and saw potential. If God can love a man like Nebuchadnezzar, what does that say about the heart of God? Discuss the last three words of 1 John 4:8: "God is love." Discuss 1 John 4:10.

5. How did God pursue you?

6. Read these verses, then discuss the question that follows: John 3:16, 18; 2 Peter 3:9; 1 Timothy 2:4. When a person dies unsaved and goes to hell for all eternity, is it God's fault? Whose fault is it?

Chapter Seven

FROM LIGHT TO DARKNESS

Daniel Chapter 5

How does a person or a nation go from spiritual light to spiritual darkness? The process really isn't complicated. It's very simple. When a person or a nation has been exposed to light, then turns toward the source of that light, that person or that nation will receive more light. When, however, an individual or a nation turns away from that light (turns away from God), then that individual or that nation will soon slip into darkness. When light is rejected and darkness ascends, divine judgment is not far away.

There is a time gap between chapters four and five of approximately twenty-three years. We know from the ancient records of secular history that many significant events took place during these years. One of those events was the death of Nebuchadnezzar. After his death, four separate kings rose to power. The first king reigned for two years, and the second king's reign lasted four years. After that, the third king, a mere child, reigned for nine months before being beaten to death by conspirators. Then, a fourth king, Nabonidus, took the throne. He reigned for seventeen difficult years. The armies of the Medes and the Persians were on the march and invaded the empire. Nabonidus appointed his son Belshazzar as a co-ruler. Belshazzar would stay in

Babylon, while Nabonidus and his army attempted to restrain the Medes and the Persians from making further military advancements within the Babylonian kingdom. Things were not going well within the kingdom. Merrill C. Tenney reports that:

> . . . there had been inflation brought on both by the continuing military expenditure and by the extensive program of public works began by Nebuchadnezzar. This amounted to 50% between 560 and 530 B.C., resulting in widespread famine.[11]

But Belshazzar and his advisors back in the city of Babylon were unconcerned. The city was considered impregnable. Herodotus, a Greek historian (fifth century BC), claimed that Babylon was built in a square with each of the four sides being fourteen miles long. His writings tell us that the outer wall, which was built around the whole city, was eighty-seven feet thick, and 350 feet high. Chariots could parade around the top abreast. He wrote that hundreds of towers were built on top of the wall at regular intervals. These towers were one hundred feet taller than the wall. Trained professional archers were on guard in those towers.

The great Euphrates River flowed from north to south right through the middle of the city of Babylon. Gates with iron bars allowed the river to flow through the city, but kept invaders out. As a further hindrance to would-be invaders, a canal was dug that surrounded the wall of the city. Inside that massive wall there was another wall, and between the two walls there was another canal for protection. Babylon was truly a magnificent city. Who among us hasn't heard of the famous "hanging gardens of Babylon?"

The streets were lined with buildings three and four stories high. The temple of Bel was eight stories high. There were farms within the city. They had plenty of food and water. If necessary, they could withstand a siege of many years.

There are several messages (or lessons) divinely placed in this chapter for our protection, for our knowledge, and for our edification. Let's consider three of these.

A Message About Godless Men—Verses 1-9

Approximately seventy years had passed since the events of chapter one. Daniel had arrived in Babylon as a teenager, but now he is an old man, somewhere around eighty-six. King Nebuchadnezzar had given him a high government position when he was a young man, but things changed after the king's death. Chapters 1-4 reveal that God had graciously given the Babylonians great light. In the years following the fourth chapter, they had turned away from that light. It was almost as if there had never been any divine light in that culture. The darkness that paganism always brings was thick in Babylon.

Belshazzar's Great Feast

The king decided to give a great feast but it would turn out to be a great fiasco! Great feasts were common in those days, but this was a dumb thing to do at this particular time. The Medes and the Persians had conquered all of the provinces of Babylon. The great Babylonian Empire was gone. All that remained was the magnificent city Babylon. This was the backdrop for Belshazzar's feast. Understand, this was not a "church social." This was an ungodly crowd. This was to be a night of music, dancing girls, overeating, and plenty of wine.

Then, Belshazzar decided to mock the God of Israel. He apparently had consumed quite a bit of wine when he had made the decision to mock God. "Wine is a mocker, strong drink is raging: and whosoever is deceived thereby is not wise" (Prov. 20:1). I can almost see the handwriting on the wall, can't you?

> Belshazzar the king made a great feast to a thousand of his lords, and drank wine before the thousand. Belshazzar, whiles he tasted the wine, commanded to bring the golden and silver vessels which his father Nebuchadnezzar had taken out of the temple which was in Jerusalem; that the king, and his princes, his wives, and his concubines, might drink therein. Then they brought the golden vessels that were taken

83

out of the temple of the house of God which was at Jerusalem; and the king, and his princes, his wives, and his concubines, drank in them. They drank wine, and praised the gods of gold, and of silver, of brass, of iron, of wood, and of stone. In the same hour came forth fingers of a man's hand, and wrote over against the candlestick upon the plaster of the wall of the king's palace: and the king saw the part of the hand that wrote.

(Dan. 5:1-5)

In the ruins of Nebuchadnezzar's palace archeologists have uncovered a large throne room 56 feet wide and 173 feet long that probably was the scene of this banquet. Midway in the long wall opposite the entrance there was a niche in front of which the king may well have been seated. The walls were washed over with white gypsum and covered in one place with a façade of ornamental bricks.[12]

Then the king's countenance was changed, and his thoughts troubled him, so that the joints of his loins were loosed, and his knees smote one against another. The king cried aloud to bring in the astrologers, the Chaldeans, and the soothsayers. And the king spake, and said to the wise men of Babylon, Whosoever shall read this writing, and shew me the interpretation thereof, shall be clothed with scarlet, and have a chain of gold about his neck, and shall be the third ruler in the kingdom. Then came in all the king's wise men: but they could not read the writing, nor make known to the king the interpretation thereof. Then was king Belshazzar greatly troubled, and his countenance was changed in him, and his lords were astonied.

(Dan. 5:6-9)

A Message About a Godly Man

Nebuchadnezzar was actually Belshazzar's grandfather. In verse two he is called his father, which was the custom of the day. Nebuchadnezzar had a daughter, and she was married to Nabonidus, and was thus a queen. She was the mother of Belshazzar. The queen in our text was no doubt his mother. She had not forgotten Daniel.

> Now the queen, by reason of the words of the king and his lords, came into the banquet house: and the queen spake and said, O king, live for ever: let not thy thoughts trouble thee, nor let thy countenance be changed: there is a man in thy kingdom, in whom is the spirit of the holy gods; and in the days of thy father light and understanding and wisdom, like the wisdom of the gods, was found in him; whom the king Nebuchadnezzar thy father, the king, I say, thy father, made master of the magicians, astrologers, Chaldeans, and soothsayers; forasmuch as an excellent spirit, and knowledge, and understanding, interpreting of dreams, and shewing of hard sentences, and dissolving of doubts, were found in the same Daniel, whom the king named Belteshazzar: now let Daniel be called, and he will shew the interpretation. Then was Daniel brought in before the king. And the king spake and said unto Daniel, Art thou that Daniel, which art of the children of the captivity of Judah, whom the king my father brought out of Jewry? I have even heard of thee, that the spirit of the gods is in thee, and that light and understanding and excellent wisdom is found in thee. And now the wise men, the astrologers, have been brought in before me, that they should read this writing, and make known unto me the interpretation thereof: but they could not shew the interpretation of the thing: And I have heard of thee, that thou canst make interpretations, and dissolve doubts: now if thou canst read the writing, and make known to me the interpretation thereof, thou shalt be clothed with scarlet, and have a chain of gold about thy neck, and shalt be the third ruler in the kingdom.
>
> (Dan. 5:10-16)

Daniel, now an old man, will once again speak to a pagan king about the true and mighty God.

> Then Daniel answered and said before the king, Let thy gifts be to thyself, and give thy rewards to another; yet I will read the writing

unto the king, and make known to him the interpretation. O thou king, the most high God gave Nebuchadnezzar thy father a kingdom, and majesty, and glory, and honour: and for the majesty that he gave him, all people, nations, and languages, trembled and feared before him: whom he would he slew; and whom he would he kept alive; and whom he would he set up; and whom he would he put down. But when his heart was lifted up, and his mind hardened in pride, he was deposed from his kingly throne, and they took his glory from him: and he was driven from the sons of men; and his heart was made like the beasts, and his dwelling was with the wild asses: they fed him with grass like oxen, and his body was wet with the dew of heaven; till he knew that the most high God ruled in the kingdom of men, and that he appointeth over it whomsoever he will.

(Dan. 5:17-21)

Belshazzar had been given light from God, but like so many others in Babylon, he didn't want the light. He turned away from it.

And thou his son, O Belshazzar, hast not humbled thine heart, though thou knewest all this; but hast lifted up thyself against the Lord of heaven; and they have brought the vessels of his house before thee, and thou, and thy lords, thy wives, and thy concubines, have drunk wine in them; and thou hast praised the gods of silver, and gold, of brass, iron, wood, and stone, which see not, nor hear, nor know: and the God in whose hand thy breath is, and whose are all thy ways, hast thou not glorified.

(Dan. 5:22-24)

A Message Directly From God

Next, Daniel interpreted the message from God to an arrogant, foolish king.

And this is the writing that was written, MENE, MENE, TEKEL, UPHARSIN. This is the interpretation of the thing: MENE; God hath numbered thy kingdom, and finished it. TEKEL; Thou art weighed in the balances, and art found wanting. PERES; Thy kingdom is divided, and given to the Medes and Persians. Then commanded Belshazzar, and they clothed Daniel with scarlet, and put a chain of gold about his neck, and made a proclamation concerning him that, he should be the third ruler in the kingdom. In that night was Belshazzar the king of the Chaldeans slain. And Darius the Median took the kingdom, being about threescore and two years old.

(Dan. 5:25-31)

Daniel does not tell us how the invaders gained entrance to the city of Babylon that night, but secular history does. Wiersbe's comments are helpful. He explains how and why.

Because of the high walls, the guard towers, and the strong bronze gates, the people in the city of Babylon thought they were safe from the enemy; but the Medo-Persian army found a way to get into the city. The Euphrates River flowed through Babylon from north to south, and by diverting the stream, the army was able to go under the city gates and into the city. The conquest of Babylon and its ultimate destruction had been predicted by Isaiah (Isa. 13-14; 21:47) and Jeremiah (Jer. 50-51). Babylon had been God's chosen instrument to chasten His people Israel, but the Babylonian army had carried things too far and mistreated the Jews (50:33-34). The conquest of Babylon was also God's punishment for what they had done to His temple. (50:28; 51:11).[13]

Herodotus, the fifth century BC Greek historian, speaks to us now through his writings:

Cyrus . . . then advanced against Babylon. But the Babylonians, having taken the field, awaited his coming; and when he had advanced near the city, the Babylonians gave battle, and, being defeated, were shut up in the city. But as they had been long aware of the restless spirit of Cyrus, and saw that he attacked all nations alike, they had laid up provisions for many years, and therefore were under no apprehensions about a siege. On the other hand, Cyrus found himself in difficulty, since much time had elapsed, and his affairs were not at all advanced. Whether, therefore, someone else made the suggestion to him in his perplexity, or whether he himself devised the plan, he had recourse to the following stratagem. Having stationed the bulk of his army near the passage of the river where it enters Babylon, and again having stationed another division beyond the city, where the river makes its exit, he gave order to his forces to enter the city as soon as they should see the stream fordable. Having stationed his forces and given these directions, he himself marched away with the ineffective part of his army; and having come to the lake, Cyrus did the same with respect to the river and the lake as the queen of the Babylonians had done; for having diverted the river, by means of a canal, into the lake, which was before a swamp, he made the ancient channel fordable by the sinking of the river. When this took place, the Persians who were appointed to that purpose close to the stream of the river, which had now subsided to about the middle of a man's thigh, entered Babylon by this passage. If, however, the Babylonians had been aware of it beforehand, or had known what Cyrus was about, they would not have suffered the Persians to enter the city, but would have utterly destroyed them; for, having shut all the little gates that lead to the river, and mounting the walls that extend along the banks of the river, they would have caught them as in a net; whereas the Persians came upon them by surprise. It is related by the people who inhabited this city, that, by reason of its great extent, when they who were at the extremities were taken, those of the Babylonians who inhabited the centre knew nothing of the capture (for it happened to be a festival); but they were dancing at the time, and enjoying themselves, till they received certain information of the truth. And thus Babylon was taken for the first time.[14]

Babylon as a nation had rejected the light that God had given her. Belshazzar also rejected the light. When a person, or a nation, has been blessed with light, but then turns away, judgment is not far away. Apply this concept to our beloved country, America. We are turning away more and more from the light. I am deeply concerned for our nation. Friend, you and I can make a difference if we will keep turning toward the light. When we are walking with the Lord, we are walking in the Light (1 John 1:7).

Questions for Discussion
or Personal Study Emphasis

1. Belshazzar and his army had underestimated the threat of the Medes and the Persians. Has that ever happened in America? Discuss. Are you concerned that this could happen in America? Discuss.

2. We are not told in Scripture how the enemy managed to gain entrance to the city of Babylon. We learn about that from secular history. Why do you think God used a secular historian to give us this information?

3. On three separate occasions Daniel recorded the failure of the "wise men" of Babylon to interpret the message of God. What point is Daniel trying to make?

4. Do you think that pride is a big issue among many in high political positions today?

5. In what ways has America turned away from the light? Discuss.

6. Name one big reason why God allowed Daniel to be delivered into the lion's den.

Chapter Eight

THE GOD OF THE AGES IS THE GOD FOR ALL AGES

Daniel Chapter 6

The God we worship, the God of Scripture, is the self-existing God. He has always been. He is the God of the ages. He made us, He loves us, and He wants to use us in His great work. He wants to use you. Let me say that again. He wants to use you. Some reading these words may think, "God can't use me; I'm too young." Someone else may think, "Not me; I'm too old."

Remember, when taken into Babylon as a captive, Daniel was a mere teenager, but God really used him. In this chapter Daniel was an old man, but God wasn't through with him. God was, in fact, about to use this aged saint once again in a big way. The same God who uses teenagers also uses senior citizens. He is the God for all ages. Friend, regardless of your age, regardless of your background, if you will make yourself available, the God of the ages can and will use you. The God of *the* ages is the God *for all* ages.

The Organization of the New Kingdom

The story in this chapter is fascinating, but it becomes even more so with a few facts that link our modern world with the ancient world of Daniel's day. The ancient city of Babylon, now just a massive site of ruins, is in modern-day Iraq. The Persians came from Persia, which is modern day Iran. The ancient Medes are the modern-day Kurds. Today they live in a region (not a country) called Kurdistan, which includes adjacent parts of Iran, Iraq, Syria, and Turkey. These places are often in the news today aren't they?

The Medes and the Persians took the kingdom by force. The Chaldean Empire of Babylon ended on October 11, 539 BC. It only lasted for approximately seventy years. The Medes and the Persians had their own law system. King Darius, the new ruler, wanted to reorganize the kingdom and implement his style of government as quickly as possible for the purpose of collecting taxes and ruling over the provinces. During these preliminary reorganization meetings, the king became very impressed with Daniel's administrative skills, his personality, his leadership ability, and with Daniel's sincere faith in his God. The king consulted with Daniel and many others from the previous empire during these days of reorganizing. The king was amazed at Daniel's skills. At every opportunity, Daniel would tell the king about his God, and the king listened respectfully. He liked Daniel and trusted him so he made Daniel the chief administrator in the entire empire.

> It pleased Darius to set over the kingdom an hundred and twenty princes, which should be over the whole kingdom; and over these three presidents; of whom Daniel was first: that the princes might give accounts unto them, and the king should have no damage. Then this Daniel was preferred above the presidents and princes, because an excellent spirit was in him; and the king thought to set him over the whole realm.
>
> (Dan. 6:1-3)

The Organizing and Execution of a Plot Against Daniel

As a new government was being formed, a plot against Daniel was planned. Some of the other government officials detested the fact that he was their superior. Graft and greed were two of the reasons why these men didn't want Daniel in power. With Daniel's watchful eye over the king's business, it would be difficult for these officials to "skim" tax revenues for their own pockets. Then too, Daniel was a Jew, and the world has long hated the Jews. Satan is behind that hatred. Satan has always hated the people of God. In Old Testament times, the Jews were the people of God.

> Then the presidents and princes sought to find occasion against Daniel concerning the kingdom; but they could find none occasion nor fault; forasmuch as he was faithful, neither was there any error or fault found in him. Then said these men, We shall not find any occasion against this Daniel, except we find it against him concerning the law of his God. Then these presidents and princes assembled together to the king, and said thus unto him, King Darius, live for ever. All the presidents of the kingdom, the governors, and the princes, the counsellors, and the captains, have consulted together to establish a royal statute, and to make a firm decree, that whosoever shall ask a petition of any God or man for thirty days, save of thee, O king, he shall be cast into the den of lions. Now, O king, establish the decree, and sign the writing, that it be not changed, according to the law of the Medes and Persians, which altereth not. Wherefore king Darius signed the writing and the decree.
>
> (Dan. 6:4-9)

They didn't consult with Daniel, so this was a lie. They might have reasoned with the king that this decree would elevate him quickly as the world leader in all of the provinces. Their suggestion would also appeal to the king's pride. I can hear these career politicians saying, "Just think, O king, if you sign this decree everybody in the world will be paying homage to you."

Notice the den of lions in verse 7. That was a form of execution used by the Medes and the Persians. Walvoord's research is helpful on the subject of ancient lions' dens:

Keil gives an interesting account of a lions' den such as has been found in more modern times., "We have no account by the ancients of the construction of lions' dens. Ge. Host, in his work on *Fez and Morocco*, p. 77, describes the lions' dens as they have been found in Morocco. According to his account, they consist of a large square cavern under the earth, having a partition-wall in the middle of it, which is furnished with a door, which the keeper can open and close from above. By throwing in food, they can entice the lions from one chamber into the other, and then, having shut the door, they enter the vacant space for the purpose of cleaning it. The cavern is open above, its mouth being surrounded by a wall of a yard and a half high, over which one can look down into the den. This description agrees perfectly with that which is here given in the text regarding the lions' den." This kind of construction would account for the fact that Darius was able to converse freely with Daniel while Daniel was still barricaded inside the den.[15]

I know what I would have done. I would have done the same thing you would have done. I would have closed the windows, locked the doors and prayed quietly in private! Daniel however didn't do that.

Now when Daniel knew that the writing was signed, he went into his house; and his windows being open in his chamber toward Jerusalem, he kneeled upon his knees three times a day, and prayed, and gave thanks before his God, as he did aforetime. Then these men assembled, and found Daniel praying and making supplication before his God. Then they came near, and spake before the king concerning the king's decree; Hast thou not signed a decree, that every man that shall ask a petition of any God or man within thirty days, save of thee, O king, shall be cast into the den of lions? The king answered and said, The thing is true, according to the law of the Medes and Persians, which altereth not. Then answered they and said before the king, That Daniel, which is of the children of the captivity of Judah, regardeth not thee, O king, nor the decree that thou hast signed, but maketh his petition three times a day. Then the king, when he heard these words, was sore displeased with himself, and set his heart on Daniel to deliver him: and he laboured till the going down of the sun to deliver him. Then these men assembled unto the king, and said unto the king, Know, O king, that the law of the Medes and Persians is, That no decree nor statute which the king establisheth may be changed.

(Dan. 6:10-15)

The Obituary of Daniel

Those wicked conspirators knew that they had Daniel. He was as good as dead. They probably had someone working on writing his obituary. As soon as they were out of the king's sight, there were "high fives" all around.

Then the king commanded, and they brought Daniel, and cast him into the den of lions. Now the king spake and said unto Daniel, Thy God whom thou servest continually, he will deliver thee. And a stone was brought, and laid upon the mouth of the den; and the king sealed it with his own signet, and with the signet of his lords; that the purpose might not be changed concerning Daniel.

(Dan. 6:16-17)

Walvoord gives us additional insight on the translation of the king's words:

The king's command was carried out and Daniel was thrown to the lions—but not before Darius made this remarkable statement to Daniel: "May your God, whom you serve continually, deliver you!" The idea is that the king was saying, "I have tried to save you but have failed. Now your God *must* save you" Daniel's personal piety and faithfulness to God had made an obvious impression on Darius, giving the king some hope that Daniel's God might come to his rescue. Goldingay believes that little can be read into the king's statement regarding whether or not he believed God would rescue Daniel.

"Darius, in turn, uses a form of the verb that leaves open whether God must, will, may, or even can rescue Daniel." However, Archer believes the king's words "voiced a tremendous hope." Verses 18-20 seem to support the idea that the king had his doubts about the ability of Daniel's God to provide deliverance. The mouth of the den was sealed with the king's signet as a token of the injunction's fulfillment. No human could interfere, not even Darius himself.[16]

Notice what they did. They placed Daniel in a cavern where the lions were kept. They rolled a stone upon the mouth of the cavern, and then it was sealed with the king's signet.

The Overpowering God

Then the king went to his palace, and passed the night fasting: neither were instruments of music brought before him: and his sleep went from him. Then the king arose very early in the morning, and went in haste unto the den of lions. And when he came to the den, he cried with a lamentable voice unto Daniel: and the king spake and said to Daniel, O Daniel, servant of the living God, is thy God, whom thou servest continually, able to deliver thee from the lions? Then said Daniel unto the king, O king, live for ever. My God hath sent his angel, and hath shut the lions' mouths, that they have not hurt me: forasmuch as before him innocency was found in me; and also before thee, O king, have I done no hurt. Then was the king exceeding glad for him, and commanded that they should take Daniel up out of the den. So Daniel was taken up out of the den, and no manner of hurt was found upon him, because he believed in his God.

(Dan. 6:18-23)

Daniel had no way of knowing what was going to happen to him that night, but the all- powerful God protected Daniel. His faith had always been strong, but it would be even stronger now. Here is what Hal Lindsey said about growing in faith:

Faith is like a muscle. Muscle only grows when you take it to the limit of its endurance. Then it will grow. Faith is exactly like that. Faith only grows when God allows you to be taken to the limit of your present maturity, then that stretches your faith and it grows.[17]

The Outcome of Daniel's Stand for Right

And the king commanded, and they brought those men which had accused Daniel, and they cast them into the den of lions, them, their children, and their wives; and the lions had the mastery of them, and brake all their bones in pieces or ever they came at the bottom of the den.

(Dan. 6:24)

This was the Middle East's idea of justice in those days. Study the cultures in the Middle East today, and you'll quickly see that things haven't changed much in 2,500 years. Next, we are going see the king converted as a direct result of Daniel's stand for God.

Then king Darius wrote unto all people, nations, and languages, that dwell in all the earth; Peace be multiplied unto you. I make a decree, That in every dominion of my kingdom men tremble and fear before the God of Daniel: for he is the living God, and stedfast for ever, and his kingdom that which shall not be destroyed, and his dominion shall be even unto the end. He delivereth and rescueth, and he worketh signs and wonders in heaven and in earth, who hath delivered Daniel from the power of the lions. So this Daniel prospered in the reign of Darius, and in the reign of Cyrus the Persian.

(Dan. 6:25-28)

Once again, in the dark pagan world of the sixth century BC, God was exalted by the testimony of a king who had been converted. What an impact that decree must have had. There was no doubt there were some "seekers" in that age who wanted to know spiritual truth. There were some faithful Jews who lived within the kingdom. God always has a remnant in this dark world. A seeker could go to a Jew who was known for being sincere, and say, "I have read the king's decree and I would like to know about Daniel's God. Will you tell me about Him?"

Daniel was born over 600 years before Christ came into our world, yet in this chapter he is a type of Christ. Consider the following:

1. Enemies conspired against him.
2. Enemies demanded his death.
3. The ruler found "no fault" in him.
4. The ruler tried to exonerate him.
5. He was placed into the tomb of the cavern.
6. The tomb was sealed.
7. There was an angel.
8. Early in the morning the stone was removed.
9. A miracle had occurred! He was supposed to be dead, but he was alive!
10. Because he lived, many others would come to saving faith also!

What an amazing God is our God. The whole story of Christ's death, burial, and resurrection was recorded here in this ancient text written 500 years before it happened! Only the living God, the God of the ages, could do that.

As a young man, Daniel was faithful to God. Because of this, Nebuchadnezzar was converted and sent his testimony to the whole world (Dan. 4:3, 35). When Darius the Mede came to power, Daniel was an old man way up in his eighties, but he was still serving God, and still willing to do whatever God wanted. He was willing, and that was the key.

God knew you before you were ever born (Ps. 22:9). He formed you when you were in your mother's womb (Isa. 44:2, Jer. 1:5). He made you, He knows you, He loves you, and He wants to use you; but you must be available. Every community has great spiritual needs. When God looks down upon your community, He sees the need. Then He asks, "Whom shall I send, and who will go . . .?" One man heard God speak these words, and with great emotion in his voice, he said to Him, "Here am I, send me" (Isa. 6:8).

That is a model prayer for all of us, and if you will sincerely pray that prayer to the God of ages, then regardless of your age, He will use you. The God of *the* ages is the God of *all* ages.

Questions for Discussion or Personal Study Emphasis

1. King Darius was impressed with Daniel. Name some of the reasons why.

2. Daniel really impacted the king's life. Do you think it is possible today for a believer to have that same kind of impact upon a lost person?

3. The government workers had sin problems. That was over 2,500 years ago. Has the human race improved? If so, how? If not, why not?

4. Does anything in this text that relates to the government workers remind you of government workers in our day?

5. In your opinion, why did God use Daniel as a type of Christ in this chapter?

6. Name one important reason why God allowed Daniel to be placed in the lions' den.

Chapter Nine

THE STORM BEFORE THE CALM

Daniel Chapter 7

The very first man and the very first woman sinned against God, their creator. The first baby born to this couple was Cain. He was, therefore, the first baby born into this world. When he grew up he murdered his brother Abel.

The history of the human race is tragic. Man's history is filled with fights, murder, conflicts and wars. All through human history, the only thing that has kept a nation from being overrun by enemies is power. Power and power alone, keeps a nation from being overtaken and ruled by others. History is filled with examples of men who were driven in their passion for power over others. Millions of people have died on the battlefields, and millions more will. Man has not and will not be able to establish universal peace on earth.

But what man cannot do, the Lord will do. When the Lord Jesus Christ returns to this troubled earth He will set up His kingdom, and then, at last, there will be peace on earth. There is, however, a terrible time of trouble coming to the people of earth before Christ comes and establishes universal peace. I call this coming time of trouble, "the storm before the calm."

Daniel's Dream

Daniel, chapter seven, has been called one of the greatest chapters of the Bible. In 553 BC, Daniel had a dream and was given a panoramic view of key future events that would serve as stepping-stones leading up to the time that Christ will set up His millennial kingdom on earth. This chapter contains a brief overview of God's program for the human race from Daniel's day to the time of Christ's second coming. Here are the kingdoms that are discussed in this chapter: the kingdoms of earth, the coming kingdom of Satan, and the coming kingdom of Christ.

Daniel Saw Four Beasts

The first thing that Daniel saw in his dream was the sea being churned up by winds from all four directions. A churning, restless sea in Scripture is often a picture of the masses of mankind, and the nations of the world (Isa. 17:12-13, 57:20; Ezek. 26:3; Rev. 17:15). One day, as a kid on the farm, I picked a little wildflower and placed it into a container of water and watched it float. Then I discovered that I could make that little flower go wherever I wanted it to go in that container by simply blowing on it. Wiersbe commented on the winds that blew on the sea as follows:

> From the human point of view, the nations seem to work out their own destinies, but the universal winds of God blow over the surface of the water to accomplish His will in His time. If there's one message that is emphasized in the book of Daniel it is that "the Most High rules in the kingdom of men" (4:32 KJV).[18]

> In the first year of Belshazzar king of Babylon Daniel had a dream and visions of his head upon his bed: then he wrote the dream, and told the sum of the matters. Daniel spake and said, I saw in my vision by night, and, behold, the four winds of the heaven strove upon the great sea. And four great beasts came up from the sea, diverse one from another.
>
> (Dan. 7:1-3)

Later in this chapter we will learn from an angel that the four beasts represented four earthly kingdoms. They are in the same order as the kingdoms were in Nebuchadnezzar's dream (chapter 2). The kingdoms in Nebuchadnezzar's dream were represented by a stunning image of man, but in Daniel's dream four beasts represented the kingdoms. Why the difference? Most Bible scholars seem to agree that Nebuchadnezzar's dream represents man's viewpoint on these kingdoms (beautiful, powerful, majestic, etc.), while Daniel's dream represents God's viewpoint of them. Wiersbe said it well when he said:

> To human eyes, the nations of the world are like Nebuchadnezzar's great image, impressive and important, but from God's viewpoint, the nations are only ferocious beasts that attack and seek to devour one another.[19]

The First Beast: Babylon

> The first was like a lion, and had eagle's wings: I beheld till the wings thereof were plucked, and it was lifted up from the earth, and made stand upon the feet as a man, and a man's heart was given to it.
>
> (Dan. 7:4)

The first beast represents the kingdom of Babylon. It corresponds to the head of gold in Nebuchadnezzar's dream (Dan. 2:37-38). The beast looked like a lion, but it had wings like an eagle. Bible teacher Dr. Ronald Showers said, "Winged lions were practically the national symbol of ancient Babylon. Sculptors of huge winged lions stand at the entrance of Babylonians royal palaces."[20] After God "plucked" Nebuchadnezzar's wings by taking his mind and making him live as a beast in the fields for seven years, He gave him back his mind, and put him back on his feet (chapter 4). After that experience Nebuchadnezzar stopped conquering and started treating the people in his kingdom better.

The Second Beast: Medo-Persia

And behold another beast, a second, like to a bear, and it raised up itself on one side, and it had three ribs in the mouth of it between the teeth of it: and they said thus unto it, Arise, devour much flesh.

(Dan. 7:5)

The bear corresponds with the arms and chest of silver in Nebuchadnezzar's dream (Dan. 2:39), and represents the Medes and the Persians. On the road to becoming a mighty empire they did "devour much flesh." Some Bible scholars think that the ribs in the bear's mouth might stand for Libya, Egypt, and Babylon. The Medes and Persians conquered all three of these nations.

The Third Beast: Greece

After this I beheld, and lo another, like a leopard, which had upon the back of it four wings of a fowl; the beast had also four heads; and dominion was given to it.

(Dan. 7:6)

This beast corresponds with the belly and the thighs of bronze in Nebuchadnezzar's dream (Dan. 2:39), and represents Alexander the Great, and the Greek Empire. Walvoord informs us that:

With the swiftness of a leopard, Alexander conquered most of the civilized world all the way from Macedonia to Africa and eastward to India. The lightning character of his conquests is without precedent in the ancient world, and this is fully in keeping with the image of speed embodied in the leopard and the four wings on its back.[21]

By 331 BC Alexander had defeated the Medes and the Persians. He died on June 13, 323 BC, at age 32. After his death, his kingdom was divided into four parts by four of his generals. The four heads of the leopard represent these divisions.

The Fourth Beast: Rome

> After this I saw in the night visions, and behold a fourth beast, dreadful
> and terrible, and strong exceedingly; and it had great iron teeth: it
> devoured and brake in pieces, and stamped the residue with the feet
> of it: and it was diverse from all the beasts that were before it; and it
> had ten horns.
>
> (Dan. 7:7)

This beast corresponds with the legs of iron in Nebuchadnezzar's
dream (Dan. 2:40-43) and represents the Roman Empire. This beast
was different from the others in Daniel's dream, in that it did not look
like any earthly animal. It also had "iron teeth." With its great military
might it could devour and crush any that stood in its path. By the year
146 BC Rome had become the world power.

The Coming Kingdom of Satan

The Roman Empire was never conquered. Over a period of hundreds
of years, it simply fell apart. But the Bible teaches the Roman Empire
nations of Europe will come together once again, form a union, and
become a modern super power. Part of the prophecy in verse seven
concerning Rome is future (yet to be fulfilled), and all of the prophecy
found in verse eight is also future (yet to be fulfilled). The ten horns
at the end of verse seven represent ten presidents of nations in Europe
who will form a confederation.

> I considered the horns, and, behold, there came up among them
> another little horn, before whom there were three of the first horns
> plucked up by the roots: and, behold, in this horn were eyes like the
> eyes of man, and a mouth speaking great things.
>
> (Dan. 7:8)

The "little horn" is another European leader who will rise to
power and have three of those presidents assassinated so that he can

rule over all of these nations. The little horn of Daniel chapter seven is known in theological circles as the Antichrist. For a short time he will rule the whole world. His rise to power will be swift. Satan will give him his power and will indwell him. This shall be the kingdom of Satan, for Satan shall rule through the Antichrist. The little horn of verse eight will hate God, and will hate the people of God. This little horn will bring a time of trouble to this earth such as has never been seen. The Bible tells us there are more wars in earth's future. The storm is coming.

But this little horn, the Antichrist, will not be revealed until the church (all believers) has been taken to heaven (2 Thess. 2:1-8). That coming great event is known as the rapture. On that blessed day, Christ shall appear in the clouds, and call us up. We will rise to meet Him in the air, and He will take us to the Father's house (John 14:1-3). The world will not realize what has taken place. After the rapture, the storm will come. What a storm it will be! Here is what Jesus said about that coming storm when the Antichrist is ruling here on earth:

> For then shall be great tribulation, such as was not since the beginning of the world to this time, no, nor ever shall be. And except those days should be shortened, there should no flesh be saved: but for the elect's sake those days shall be shortened.
>
> (Matt. 24:21-22)

The coming storm is the tribulation period mentioned here by Jesus Christ. When He returns to earth the nations will be involved in a great and awful war in the Middle East. The focus of that war will be Jerusalem and the land of Israel. Christ will put an end to the wars. He will destroy the enemies of His people, and then He will set up His kingdom. Peace is coming to earth, but not at the hand of man. Christ will establish peace.

Our Lord has many titles in Scripture, and each one of those titles is precious to those of us who love Him. One of His titles is Prince of

Peace. When Christ rules on earth, there will be universal peace. If Christ is in your life, you can have His peace today. How? By letting Him rule. For 2000 years Christ has been putting out storms in people's lives. He replaces their confusion, their trouble, and their sins with His peace. When He is ruling in our hearts, we have peace.

Questions for Discussion
or Personal Study Emphasis

1. God used beasts in Daniel's dream to represent the kingdoms of man and to reveal their nature. How does man's view of these kingdoms differ from God's view?

2. If God used images of beasts to picture the kingdoms of man, what does that teach us about our race? Do any scriptures come to mind?

3. What does modern man think of himself?

4. What do you know about the coming world power that is described in the Bible?

5. Who will be the earthly leader of that coming world power? What do you know about him?

6. Will there ever be a lasting peace on earth? Scripture?

Chapter Ten

THE COMING WORLD LEADER

Daniel 7:9-28

Current events in many nations make it clear to the serious Bible prophecy student that the church age is going to end soon. The church age will end when Christ comes to get His church. The church is all of those who have put their faith in Christ as their Savior. When Jesus appears in the sky, the Bible states that we will rise "to meet the Lord in the air: and so shall we ever be with the Lord" (1 Thess. 4:17).

After the rapture of the church, there will come a time of trouble to the people of earth called the tribulation. The tribulation period will only last seven years, but it will be the darkest time in all of human history. We see our world getting darker by the day. It seems that every right thing is being cast aside, and every wrong thing is being promoted and exalted. We may very well experience Christian persecution in America before the rapture occurs. Believers in Christ have been persecuted ever since the church began 2,000 years ago.

God has given us prophecy because there are things He wants us to know. One of the things He wants us to know is this: we are on the winning side. God wants us to know that no matter how bad things may get, because we are on the Lord's side, we are on the winning side. Ultimately, we win. Satan, the enemy of all mankind, loses.

Daniel Saw the Throne Room—Verses 9-10

After the "dream scene" of the four frightening beasts (vv. 1-8), the scene in Daniel's dream shifts to heaven. Daniel looked into the throne room, and was amazed as he saw God.

> Beheld till the thrones were cast down, and the Ancient of days did sit, whose garment was white as snow, and the hair of his head like the pure wool: his throne was like the fiery flame, and his wheels as burning fire.
>
> (Dan. 7:9)

"But," someone asks, "doesn't the Bible say somewhere that, 'no man has seen God at any time?'" (John 1:18; 1 John 4:12). God is spirit (John 4:24). He doesn't wear a white robe, and He doesn't have white hair. The reconciliation of Daniel's throne-room scene and the other scriptures follow. When Jesus was here on earth, He was God in the flesh. When people looked upon Jesus they looked upon God in a body. When Daniel looked into the throne room, he too, saw God in a body. Notice God's throne:

> His throne was like the fiery flame, and his wheels as burning fire. A fiery stream issued and came forth from before him: thousand thousands ministered unto him, and ten thousand times ten thousand stood before him: the judgment was set, and the books were opened.
>
> (Dan. 7:9b-10)

The Heavenly Throne of the Father—Verses 9-12

What a sight! Daniel saw a stream of fire flowing out from that throne. He apparently saw a million angels ministering to God, and one hundred million saints standing before Him. Wiersbe explained Daniel's throne room vision as follows:

The vision of God's throne parallels Ezekiel 1:15-21, 26-27. The fire speaks of His holiness and judgment against sin and the wheels symbolize His providential working in the world in ways we can't understand. "Our God is a consuming fire" (Deut. 4:24; Heb. 12:29; see Ps. 97:1-4). He is praised by a multitude of saints and angels (Rev. 5:11) as the books are opened and the Lord prepares to judge evil on the earth. No matter what Satan and the Antichrist do on earth, God is still on the throne and He executes judgment.[22]

Daniel Saw the Beasts Lose Their Authority—Verses 11-12

In the next "dream scene," Daniel saw the first three beasts lose their power, and he saw the fourth beast slain, and its body thrown into a burning flame.

> I beheld then because of the voice of the great words which the horn spake: I beheld even till the beast was slain, and his body destroyed, and given to the burning flame. As concerning the rest of the beasts, they had their dominion taken away: but their lives were prolonged for a season and time.
>
> (Dan. 7:11-12)

Walvoord explains this as follows:

> Verse 12 is saying is that the Babylonian, Medo-Persian, and Greek Empires were to some extent continued in their successors; that is, Gentile power shifted as to rulership, but continued more or less in the same pattern: thus the statement, "their dominion was taken away, but, their lives were prolonged for a season and a time." By contrast at the second coming of Christ the fourth empire is destroyed, and a totally different kingdom from heaven succeeds it. This is borne out by the image of chapter 2, as Driver notes, "the entire image remains intact until the stone falls upon the feet (representing the fourth and last kingdom), when the whole of it breaks up together." When Medo-Persia followed Babylon, the dominion of Babylon was taken

away, but in some sense the lives of the participants were prolonged. The same is true when Greece succeeded Medo-Persia and when Rome succeeded Greece. But the end of the fourth beast is to be dramatic, cataclysmic, and final. Both the rulers and the people involved are to be destroyed. As noted this interpretation agrees with Revelation 19:19-20, which records the beast as destroyed in the lake of fire and his followers struck down at the second coming of Christ. It is confirmed by Matthew 25:31-46, which records the judgment of the nations at Christ's return."[23]

Daniel was puzzled. He did not understand what these beasts represented.

Daniel Saw the Father Give the Son the Rule of the Earth—Verses 13-14

The next "dream scene" focuses on the throne room of heaven once again. In that scene Daniel saw someone approach God on His throne. Daniel described him as "one like the son of man." Later when Jesus came to earth, He called Himself, "The Son of Man." That title is found in the gospels eighty-two times. In this scene, God the Father apparently told Christ the Son to return to earth and set up His kingdom. Daniel was somehow made to realize that this kingdom would last forever.

> I saw in the night visions, and, behold, one like the Son of man came with the clouds of heaven, and came to the Ancient of days, and they brought him near before him. And there was given him dominion, and glory, and a kingdom, that all people, nations, and languages, should serve him: his dominion is an everlasting dominion, which shall not pass away, and his kingdom that which shall not be destroyed.
>
> (Dan. 7:13-14)

This event, of course, is still future, but it is going to happen. God has promised in His Holy Word that the kingdom of heaven is coming. Lehman Strauss explains:

> This is the climax of the vision presenting the goal of all history. The Son of God comes from Heaven and is invested with authority to take the kingdoms of earth from the Gentiles and to establish His kingdom. His coming as seen by Daniel is the fulfillment of a promise found in the first Messianic psalm where the Ancient of Days says to the Son, "Ask of Me, and I shall give Thee the heathen for Thine inheritance, and the uttermost parts of the earth for Thy possession" (Psalm 2:8). Daniel sees the triumph of Christ and His kingdom over all other kingdoms. He comes in power and great glory as depicted in such passages as Matthew 24 and 25; Mark 14:61-62; Luke 1:32; 2 Thessalonians 2:6-10; Revelation 19 and 20:1-4. The most casual reading of the prophetic Scriptures present clearly the coming kingdom of Christ on the earth, and the most careful scrutiny of these same Scriptures leaves no room whatever to deny His coming and His kingdom. We will not here attempt to present any of the features of this glorious kingdom. The important thing to notice is that He comes with power and authority. Daniel speaks of this event not less than five times in chapter seven (vs. 14, 18, 22, 25, 27). Daniel sees Him coming "with the clouds of heaven" (7:13). Both in the Old and New Testaments the clouds are seen frequently accompanying Him. They represent the divine presence, thus they follow Him as His mark of identification. The student should examine the following passages: Exodus 13:21; 19:9; 24:16; 34:5; Leviticus 16:2; 1 Kings 8:10; Psalm 18:11-12, 78:14, 97:2-4; Isaiah 19:1; Jeremiah 4:13; Ezekiel 10:4; Nahum 1:3; Matthew 17:5, 24:30; Luke 21:27; 1 Thessalonians 4:17; Revelation 1:7, 14:14.[24]

Daniel Asked an Angel to Explain All He Had Seen—Verses 15-22

Daniel was very troubled with the dream that he was having—especially by the fourth beast he saw. Then Daniel asked someone who was standing near (we suppose an angel) to explain the things he had just seen. The unidentified heavenly helper then explained that the four beasts represented the four kings (kingdoms), and that after the four kingdoms, the "saints" (believers) would have a kingdom that would last forever. Daniel then asked the angel to explain the fourth beast, the one that had the horn with eyes and a mouth speaking great things. That fourth beast was the one that really troubled Daniel because this was the one Daniel saw slaughtering the saints of God. He saw men and women of faith being slaughtered by the little horn.

> I Daniel was grieved in my spirit in the midst of my body, and the visions of my head troubled me. I came near unto one of them that stood by, and asked him the truth of all this. So he told me, and made me know the interpretation of the things. These great beasts, which are four, are four kings, which shall arise out of the earth. But the saints of the most High shall take the kingdom, and possess the kingdom for ever, even for ever and ever. Then I would know the truth of the fourth beast, which was diverse from all the others, exceeding dreadful, whose teeth were of iron, and his nails of brass; which devoured, brake in pieces, and stamped the residue with his feet; and of the ten horns that were in his head, and of the other which came up, and before whom three fell; even of that horn that had eyes, and a mouth that spake very great things, whose look was more stout than his fellows. I beheld, and the same horn made war with the saints, and prevailed against them; until the Ancient of days came, and judgment was given to the saints of the most High; and the time came that the saints possessed the kingdom.
>
> (Dan. 7:15-22)

Daniel Learned About the Coming World Leader—Verses 23-25

Then the angel gave Daniel a brief description of the last world empire, and of the coming last world ruler, the Antichrist. Wiersbe said, "the Greek prefix *anti* can mean 'against' and 'instead of.' The final ruler will be both a counterfeit Christ and an enemy who is against Christ."

> Thus he said, The fourth beast shall be the fourth kingdom upon earth, which shall be diverse from all kingdoms, and shall devour the whole earth, and shall tread it down, and break it in pieces.
>
> (Dan. 7:23)

This verse was fulfilled in history by the Roman Empire. It did all the things that were prophesied in this verse. There is a gap between verse 23 and verse 24 of hundreds of years. The Roman Empire lost its power hundreds of years ago. The nations of Europe, however, are no longer fighting each other as they used to. They have come back together as a "union." This modern-day union began with a document called "The Treaty of Rome." Out of this "new" Roman Empire will come the Antichrist.

Verse 24 is still future. Notice the beast suddenly has ten horns. They represent leaders of nations in Europe. Instead of one ruler like old Rome had, the new Rome will have ten, that is until the antichrist rises and takes control of the government.

> And the ten horns out of this kingdom are ten kings that shall arise: and another shall rise after them; and he shall be diverse from the first, and he shall subdue three kings. And he shall speak great words against the most High, and shall wear out the saints of the most High, and think to change times and laws: and they shall be given into his hand until a time and times and the dividing of time.
>
> (Dan. 7:24-25)

What the Coming World Leader (the Antichrist) Will Do

Here is a quick overview of what the coming world leader will do. He will wear down the tribulation saints (v. 25). He will declare war on these post-rapture believers (v. 21). He will speak against the God of the Bible (vs. 25). He will fool people with his lies (v. 11, 25; Rev. 13:5-6). He will demand and receive worship (1 Thess. 2:3-4; Rev. 13:5-8, 15-17). His reign of terror will last three-and-a-half years (Dan. 7:25; Rev. 11:2-3, 12:6, 14, 13:5). His authority will be incredible (Dan. 7:25; Rev. 13:2, 15-17). Religious liberty will not exist. He will demand that everyone worship him. Freedom of choice will not exist. He will force everyone to take the infamous "mark" either in the forehead or the hand (Rev. 13:16-17). He will get his power from Satan (Rev. 12:9, 13:4).

Daniel Again Told About the Coming Kingdom of Our Lord—Verses 26-28

The angel proceeds to tell Daniel that the Antichrist's kingdom will come to an end. When Christ comes to set up His kingdom, the Antichrist will be cast alive into the lake of fire (Rev. 19:20).

> But the judgment shall sit, and they shall take away his dominion, to consume and to destroy it unto the end. And the kingdom and dominion, and the greatness of the kingdom under the whole heaven, shall be given to the people of the saints of the most High, whose kingdom is an everlasting kingdom, and all dominions shall serve and obey him. Hitherto is the end of the matter. As for me Daniel, my cogitations much troubled me, and my countenance changed in me: but I kept the matter in my heart.
>
> (Dan. 7:26-28)

Daniel's dream came to an end. But all that he saw alarmed him; it was overwhelming. It is important that we not overlook something that God is stressing in this chapter—His coming kingdom. Four times in this chapter the Lord told Daniel that His kingdom is coming (v. 14, 18, 22, 27).

The Winning Side

If God had not included these references in the text, this chapter would be totally depressing. This question often comes up: "Will we face serious persecution in America?" We don't know, but we very well could. In many parts of the world, Christians today are being persecuted. I suggest that we be mentally prepared for the persecution that *might* come, as we wait eagerly for Jesus Christ who *is* coming.

Christ could come for us at any time. There is nothing in the Bible that has to happen before the rapture. All of the end-time prophecies deal with things that will occur on the earth after the rapture. God put end-time prophecy in the Bible so we can know where things are headed, and so we can know who wins and who loses.

Christian, when you accepted Christ as your Savior you changed teams. You are not on the losing team anymore. You are on the Lord's side. You are on the winning side. Ultimately, Jesus Christ will see to that! That deceiver named Satan will lose, and so will the Antichrist. I know it doesn't look like it now. All of us, without exception, struggle with the problems of this life, but God's Word is true. He always keeps His promises. He is the ultimate promise keeper. I'm glad that I am on His side. If you have accepted Christ, you are on His side too!

Questions for Discussion or Personal Study Emphasis

1. Name as many characteristics of the coming Antichrist as you can. Discuss.

2. The Antichrist is not in power yet, but the spirit of the Antichrist is here now (see 1 John 4:3). What evidence do you see of this statement?

3. Do you think that the spirit of the Antichrist is preparing the way for the coming Antichrist?

4. How have the nations of Europe changed in the past one hundred years? Why is this significant in light of Bible prophecy concerning the fourth beast and the "little horn"?

5. How has the nation of Israel changed in the past century? Where were the Jews before 1948? Why are they back in the land of Israel?

6. What fact impressed you the most in Daniel chapter 7?

SECTION III

THE PROPHETIC PLAN
FOR ISRAEL

Chapter Eleven

THE VISION OF THE
RAM AND THE GOAT

Daniel Chapter 8

One day in Bible college, a professor made a statement so profound it took me a while to process it. He said, "Every decision that we make is either *for* or *against* Jesus Christ." Decision making is serious business. The most important decisions we make in life are the deliberate decisions that we make concerning Jesus Christ. We see some striking examples of this in Scripture. Daniel, for example, repeatedly made decisions that honored the Lord. Decisions others consistently made in chapter eight were against the Lord. Future rewards for the saved and future punishment for the unsaved will be based upon the decisions people make in life.

Daniel Saw a Ram With Two Horns

The events in this chapter took place in 551 BC. We know this because Daniel provided us with dates as he wrote. All of the text from Daniel 2:4 through 7:28 was written in Aramaic. The emphasis in these chapters is on the Gentile nations. There is a language shift in 8:1 back to Hebrew. Daniel wrote in Hebrew from there to the end of the book. There is an *emphasis shift* here also. In the earlier revelations Daniel wrote about the emphasis was upon the Gentile nations; beginning in chapter eight, the emphasis is on Israel. The Gentiles are still in the text but the emphasis is on Israel. Daniel had a vision and then God sent the angel Gabriel to explain this vision.

> In the third year of the reign of king Belshazzar a vision appeared unto me, even unto me Daniel, after that which appeared unto me at the first. And I saw in a vision; and it came to pass, when I saw, that I was at Shushan in the palace, which is in the province of Elam; and I saw in a vision, and I was by the river of Ulai. Then I lifted up mine eyes, and saw, and, behold, there stood before the river a ram which had two horns: and the two horns were high; but one was higher than the other, and the higher came up last. I saw the ram pushing westward, and northward, and southward; so that no beasts might stand before him, neither was there any that could deliver out of his hand; but he did according to his will, and became great.
>
> (Dan. 8:1-4)

Gabriel would later tell Daniel who this ram represented: "The ram which thou sawest having two horns are the kings of Media and Persia" (Dan. 8:20). Shushan was a city roughly 200 miles southwest of Babylon. It wasn't a very significant city under the Babylonians, but under Persian rule it replaced Babylon as the capital. Wiersbe said, "Since Daniel was about to describe the victory of the Medes and the Persians over the Babylonians, God put him into the future capital of the Persian Empire."[25]

Daniel Saw a Goat With One Horn

On two previous occasions, God gave Daniel a panoramic view of the empires that would succeed Babylon. In this chapter Daniel is given a few more details, and for the first time, God names the coming kingdoms. The Medes (the smaller horn) and the Persians (the larger horn) would overtake Babylon.. History confirms the accuracy of this prophecy. Then Daniel saw a one-horned goat coming from the west. That goat had one thing on his mind: he was determined to defeat the ram (the Medes and the Persians).

> And as I was considering, behold, an he goat came from the west on the face of the whole earth, and touched not the ground: and the goat had a notable horn between his eyes. And he came to the ram that had two horns, which I had seen standing before the river, and ran unto him in the fury of his power. And I saw him come close unto the ram, and he was moved with anger against him, and smote the ram, and brake his two horns: and there was no power in the ram to stand before him, but he cast him down to the ground, and stamped upon him: and there was none that could deliver the ram out of his hand.
>
> (Dan. 8:5-7)

Gabriel would later tell Daniel who this goat represented: "And the rough goat is the king of Grecia: and the great horn that is between his eyes is the first king" (Dan. 8:21). We know from history that Greece did indeed defeat the Medes and the Persians, and their first king was Alexander the Great. His conquests started in Greece, and then he quickly came out of the west and into the east, conquering everything in his path. The Persian Empire fell in 331 BC. That was 220 years after God gave the prophecy to Daniel.

Then, in his vision, Daniel saw that the "horn" (Alexander) would be broken. Gabriel would later explain the meaning of this to Daniel. Here is what Daniel saw, followed by Gabriel's explanation: "Therefore the he goat waxed very great: and when he was strong, the great horn was broken; and for it came up four notable ones toward the four winds of heaven" (Dan. 8:8). "Now that being broken, whereas four stood up for it, four kingdoms shall stand up out of the nation, but not in his power" (Dan. 8:22).

Alexander died at age thirty-three. His vast empire was divided up among four of his generals. The four "horns" that came up after the great horn was broken represent those four generals.

Daniel Saw a Little Horn

One of these four kingdoms was Syria. The eight king of that Syrian dynasty was Antiochus Epiphanes. He reigned from 175–164 BC. He was an antichrist, and was a picture of the Antichrist who is yet to come. He even claimed he was a god. He prohibited the Jews from practicing their religion, he desecrated the temple in Jerusalem by sacrificing a pig on the altar, and he put an end to the daily sacrifice in the temple. Antiochus Epiphanes died in 164 BC during a military campaign in Media. Soon after that, the Jewish altar was cleansed and the daily sacrifice was resumed.

> And out of one of them came forth a little horn, which waxed exceeding great, toward the south, and toward the east, and toward the pleasant land. And it waxed great, even to the host of heaven; and it cast down some of the host and of the stars to the ground, and stamped upon them. Yea, he magnified himself even to the prince of the host, and by him the daily sacrifice was taken away, and the place of his sanctuary was cast down. And an host was given him against the daily sacrifice by reason of transgression, and it cast down the truth to the ground; and it practised, and prospered. Then I heard one saint speaking, and another saint said unto that certain saint which spake, How long shall be the vision concerning the daily sacrifice, and the transgression of desolation, to give both the sanctuary and the host to be trodden under foot? And he said unto me, Unto two thousand and three hundred days; then shall the sanctuary be cleansed.
>
> (Dan. 8:9-14)

Daniel Heard About a Coming Wicked King

Antiochus Epiphanes was a type or a foreshadow of the yet to come Antichrist. Daniel had this vision in 551 BC. Antiochus ruled from 175-164 BC. God told Daniel of this ruthless ruler nearly 400 years before He came!

THE VISION OF THE RAM AND THE GOAT

Finally Gabriel, God's messenger, told Daniel of an event still to come. This prophecy was given over 2,500 years ago. It deals with the coming Antichrist. You can always identify the Antichrist in Scripture because he is the one who Christ will destroy at His second coming.

> And in the latter time of their kingdom, when the transgressors are come to the full, a king of fierce countenance, and understanding dark sentences, shall stand up. And his power shall be mighty, but not by his own power: and he shall destroy wonderfully, and shall prosper, and practice, and shall destroy the mighty and the holy people.
>
> (Dan. 8:23-24)

Notice when he comes he will have great power, but it will not be his own power. Revelation chapter 13 tells us from where he will get his power.

> And I stood upon the sand of the sea, and saw a beast rise up out of the sea, having seven heads and ten horns, and upon his horns ten crowns, and upon his heads the name of blasphemy. And the beast which I saw was like unto a leopard, and his feet were as the feet of a bear, and his mouth as the mouth of a lion: and the dragon gave him his power, and his seat, and great authority.
>
> (Rev. 13:1-2)

The dragon is identified in Revelation 12:9. It is Satan. The coming Antichrist will get his power, his throne, and great authority from Satan. Notice in Daniel 8:24 who he will destroy: "the mighty and the holy people." These are the ones who will be saved after the rapture, during the early part of the tribulation, thus we call them "tribulation saints." Revelation 13:7 tells us, "And it was given unto him to make war with the saints, and to overcome them: and power was given him over all kindreds, and tongues, and nations."

Notice in Daniel 8:25 the coming world leader will stand up against Jesus Christ, the "Prince of Princes." That will be the end of him. Revelation 19 tells us about that coming event.

And I saw heaven opened, and behold a white horse; and he that sat upon him was called Faithful and True, and in righteousness he doth judge and make war. His eyes were as a flame of fire, and on his head were many crowns; and he had a name written, that no man knew, but he himself. And he was clothed with a vesture dipped in blood: and his name is called The Word of God. And the armies which were in heaven followed him upon white horses, clothed in fine linen, white and clean.

(Rev. 19:11-14)

And I saw the beast, and the kings of the earth, and their armies, gathered together to make war against him that sat on the horse, and against his army. And the beast was taken, and with him the false prophet that wrought miracles before him, with which he deceived them that had received the mark of the beast, and them that worshipped his image. These both were cast alive into a lake of fire burning with brimstone.

(Rev. 19:19-20)

It will not be a very glorious ending for the one who will force the entire world to worship him, will it?

Daniel Took a Well-Deserved "Sick Leave"

"And I Daniel fainted, and was sick certain days; afterward I rose up, and did the king's business; and I was astonished at the vision, but none understood it" (Dan. 8:27).

Important Decisions in Life

The most important decisions in life are the decisions that a person makes concerning Jesus Christ. Rejecting Jesus Christ, for example, is the absolute worst decision that a person can make. Jesus is "the way, the truth, and the life" and nobody can go to heaven without Him (John 14:6). "Every decision that we make is either for Christ or against Christ,"[26] said Dr. Mark G. Cambron.

During the coming tribulation a wicked person will rise to power in Europe, and every decision that he makes will be *against* Jesus Christ. The decisions that we make concerning Jesus Christ are life's most important decisions because they have eternal consequences. When Christ comes to earth to set up His kingdom, this wicked man will be thrown alive into the burning flame and will suffer eternal torment.

The greatest decision that a person can make is to "believe on the Lord Jesus Christ," and be saved (Acts 16:31). That is the greatest and grandest decision of life. Another important decision is to let Christ, your Savior, also be the Lord of your life. He takes control when we humbly submit to Him (Rom. 12:1-2). If you are saved, He wants you to live for Him. He will use you in surprising ways if you will simply and sincerely say to Him, "Here am I, Lord. Take control of my life. I'm willing to do whatever You want me to do."

Questions for Discussion
or Personal Study Emphasis

1. Antiochus Epiphanes persecuted the Jews terribly. Discuss some of the reasons why the Jews have been so often persecuted in the world.

2. List the ways that Antiochus pictured the coming Antichrist.

3. The coming Antichrist will receive his power, his throne, and his authority from Satan (Rev. 13:2). Study Ephesians 6:12 and then discuss or research the following question: Is Satan active in the politics of nations today?

4. Why would Satan be interested in the politics of men?

5. What is Satan's ultimate goal?

6. If it is true that the most important decisions in life are the decisions we make concerning Jesus Christ, then what are some decisions that America, as a nation, has made that have put us into such sad shape?

7. What decisions could America, as a nation, make that would get us out of this mess?

Chapter Twelve

THE PROPHECY OF THE SEVENTY WEEKS

Daniel Chapter 9

If you know Jesus Christ as your Savior, you are blessed. You will never be alone, you can talk to Him and He will help you with the problems of life, and when your life is over, you will go to be with Him.

Rejecting Christ, however, always ends in disaster. The person who rejects Christ walks alone, he doesn't have the Lord to guide him and help him with the problems of life, and when he dies, he will be separated from the Lord for all eternity in the lake of fire.

Two thousand years ago, the Messiah, Jesus Christ, came to earth, to Israel. With signs and wonders He proved He was the Son of God. Some accepted Him, believed in Him, and rejoiced in Him. But the Jewish leaders did not. If they had accepted Him as their Messiah, He would have set up His kingdom, the one the prophets spoke of. But, they rejected the Messiah, and had Him crucified. The results were tragic. Their beloved city, Jerusalem, was destroyed, their temple was destroyed, and they lost their nation. They became a people without a country.

Rejecting Christ always brings disaster, but following Christ brings joy, direction, peace, and fulfillment.

The Lord told the prophet Ezekiel He would one day bring the Jews home to their land. God would bring them back at the appointed time to the land of Israel, still in their unbelief. Almighty God said, "I will take you from among the nations, and gather you out of all countries and will bring you into your own land" (Ezek. 36:24). A few years ago that happened. After nearly 1,900 years of exile, the Jewish people have a home. Her neighbors hate her and are always plotting ways to destroy her. The Jews long for peace but they live in Israel today under the constant threat of war.

Daniel's Intense Study of the Scriptures

Because of unconfessed and unrepented sin, God allowed the Babylonians to take the Jews captive. Daniel was just a teenager, maybe sixteen years of age when he was taken captive into Babylon. He faithfully served the Lord in Babylon, and the Lord blessed him for it. Daniel is now an elderly man around eighty-three years old. As the chapter opens, we will see Daniel studying the writings of Jeremiah the prophet. Daniel's study became intense. God was teaching him some things about the capture that he did not know. Jeremiah had prophesied that after seventy years of captivity in Babylon, God would bring the Jews back home! The prophet Jeremiah had been taken captive into Egypt, yet somehow the inspired words that God had him write "found their way across desert and mountain to faraway Babylon and fell into the hands of Daniel."[27] In his study that day, Daniel read these words:

> And this whole land shall be a desolation, and an astonishment; and these nations shall serve the king of Babylon seventy years. And it shall come to pass, when seventy years are accomplished, that I will punish the king of Babylon, and that nation, saith the LORD, for their iniquity, and the land of the Chaldeans, and will make it perpetual desolations.
>
> (Jer. 25:11-12)

> For thus saith the LORD, That after seventy years be accomplished at Babylon I will visit you, and perform my good word toward you,

in causing you to return to this place. For I know the thoughts that I think toward you, saith the LORD, thoughts of peace, and not of evil, to give you an expected end. Then shall ye call upon me, and ye shall go and pray unto me, and I will hearken unto you. And ye shall seek me, and find me, when ye shall search for me with all your heart. And I will be found of you, saith the LORD: and I will turn away your captivity, and I will gather you from all the nations, and from all the places whither I have driven you, saith the LORD; and I will bring you again into the place whence I caused you to be carried away captive.

(Jer. 29:10-14)

We know all of this because Daniel himself told us.

In the first year of Darius the son of Ahasuerus, of the seed of the Medes, which was made king over the realm of the Chaldeans; In the first year of his reign I Daniel understood by books the number of the years, whereof the word of the LORD came to Jeremiah the prophet, that he would accomplish seventy years in the desolations of Jerusalem.

(Dan. 9:1-2)

Daniel's Intercessory Prayer

Daniel, surprised and amazed, probably read these verses over and over again. He must have thought, *We've been here in Babylon for around sixty-seven years, that means in three years or less, God is going to take us home! Home to Jerusalem! I must pray to the Lord for my nation, and confess to Him our national sins.* After Daniel's time of intense study, he spent some time in intercessory prayer. Intercessory prayer is praying to God on behalf of others. Daniel, I think, shed a lot of tears that day as he prayed for his nation.

Every believer in this nation should be praying for America. We have lost our way! Our sins are great, and I don't see any signs of our once-great nation turning back to God. Americans are arrogantly strutting their way down a path that leads to a swift judgment from God! I am afraid that the epitaph for many Christians in America might well be: "I watched my nation fall. I shed not a tear; I prayed not a prayer; I did not a thing except watch while my nation fell." Everyone should take some time and not just read Daniel's prayer, but to also study it. Here is his prayer:

> And I set my face unto the Lord God, to seek by prayer and supplications, with fasting, and sackcloth, and ashes: and I prayed unto the LORD my God, and made my confession, and said, O Lord, the great and dreadful God, keeping the covenant and mercy to them that love him, and to them that keep his commandments; we have sinned, and have committed iniquity, and have done wickedly, and have rebelled, even by departing from thy precepts and from thy judgments: neither have we hearkened unto thy servants the prophets, which spake in thy name to our kings, our princes, and our fathers, and to all the people of the land. O Lord, righteousness belongeth unto thee, but unto us confusion of faces, as at this day; to the men of Judah, and to the inhabitants of Jerusalem, and unto all Israel, that are near, and that are far off, through all the countries whither thou hast driven them, because of their trespass that they have trespassed against thee. O Lord, to us belongeth confusion of face, to our kings, to our princes, and to our fathers, because we have sinned against thee. To the Lord our God belong mercies and forgivenesses, though we have rebelled against him; neither have we obeyed the voice of the LORD our God, to walk in his laws, which he set before us by his servants the prophets. Yea, all Israel have transgressed thy law, even by departing, that they might not obey thy voice; therefore the curse is poured upon us, and the oath that is written in the law of Moses the servant of God, because we have sinned against him. And he hath confirmed his words, which he spake against us, and against our judges that judged us, by bringing upon us a great evil: for under the whole heaven hath not been done as hath been done upon Jerusalem. As it is written in the law of Moses, all this evil is come upon us: yet made we not our prayer before the LORD our God, that we might turn from our iniquities, and understand thy truth. Therefore hath the LORD

watched upon the evil, and brought it upon us: for the LORD our God is righteous in all his works which he doeth: for we obeyed not his voice. And now, O Lord our God, that hast brought thy people forth out of the land of Egypt with a mighty hand, and hast gotten thee renown, as at this day; we have sinned, we have done wickedly. O Lord, according to all thy righteousness, I beseech thee, let thine anger and thy fury be turned away from thy city Jerusalem, thy holy mountain: because for our sins, and for the iniquities of our fathers, Jerusalem and thy people are become a reproach to all that are about us. Now therefore, O our God, hear the prayer of thy servant, and his supplications, and cause thy face to shine upon thy sanctuary that is desolate, for the Lord's sake. O my God, incline thine ear, and hear; open thine eyes, and behold our desolations, and the city which is called by thy name: for we do not present our supplications before thee for our righteousnesses, but for thy great mercies. O Lord, hear; O Lord, forgive; O Lord, hearken and do; defer not, for thine own sake, O my God: for thy city and thy people are called by thy name.

(Dan. 9:3-19)

Daniel's Incredible Revelation

While Daniel was praying, God sent Gabriel the angel to him once again. Gabriel revealed to Daniel some things about the future of his nation, the city of Jerusalem, the temple, the Messiah, and the coming Antichrist.

And whiles I was speaking, and praying, and confessing my sin and the sin of my people Israel, and presenting my supplication before the LORD my God for the holy mountain of my God; yea, whiles I was speaking in prayer, even the man Gabriel, whom I had seen in the vision at the beginning, being caused to fly swiftly, touched me about the time of the evening oblation. And he informed me, and talked with me, and said, O Daniel, I am now come forth to give thee skill and understanding. At the beginning of thy supplications the commandment came forth, and I am come to shew thee; for thou

143

art greatly beloved: therefore understand the matter, and consider the vision.

(Dan. 9:20-23)

The Prophecy of the Seventy Weeks

We will see the number seven used repeatedly in these verses. Seven is the number of completion and perfection. Seven is God's number. With the seventy-year captivity about to end, God gives Daniel an overview of future events relating to Israel. Daniel learns that after the seventy-year captivity another "seventy" would begin.

> Seventy weeks are determined upon thy people and upon thy holy city, to finish the transgression, and to make an end of sins, and to make reconciliation for iniquity, and to bring in everlasting righteousness, and to seal up the vision and prophecy, and to anoint the most Holy.
>
> (Dan. 9:24)

The Hebrew word for weeks used here is *shabuwa* and it means a "seven." Gabriel was speaking about seventy periods of time of seven years each. That is 490 years. Wiersbe said:

> Gabriel explained that during those 490 years, the Lord would accomplish six specific purposes for the Jewish people. The first three have to do with sin and the last three with righteousness. The Lord would "finish the transgression," that is, the transgression of the Jewish people, and "make an end of" Israel's national sins. This was one of the main burdens of Daniel's prayer. Israel was a scattered suffering nation because she was a sinful nation. How would the Lord accomplish this? By making "reconciliation for iniquity," that is, by offering a sacrifice that would atone for their sin. Here we come to the cross of Jesus Christ, Israel's Messiah. When Jesus died on the cross, He died for the sins of the whole world, (1 John 2:2; John 1:29), and therefore we can proclaim the good news of the gospel to sinners everywhere. But He also died for the church (Eph. 5:25) and

144

for the people of Israel. "For the transgression of my people was he stricken" (Isa. 53:8). Jesus died for sinners in every tribe and nation (Rev. 5:9; 7:9), but in a very special way, He died for His own people, the Jewish nation (John 11:44-52). The last three divine purposes focus on righteousness and the future kingdom of Messiah. When Jesus returns, He will establish His righteous kingdom (Jer. 23:5-6; 31:31-34) and rule in righteousness (Isa. 4:2-6). In that day, the Old Testament prophecies of Israel's glorious kingdom will be fulfilled, and there will be no need for visions or prophets. "To anoint the most Holy" refers to the sanctifying of the future temple that is described in Ezekiel 40 – 48. These six purposes declare the answers to Daniel's prayer! Ultimately, Israel's sins will be forgiven (Zech. 12:10-13:1), the city of Jerusalem will be rebuilt, and the temple and its ministry will be restored, all because of the atoning death of Jesus Christ on the cross. All of these wonderful accomplishments will be fulfilled during the 490 years that Gabriel goes on to explain. He divides the seven sevens – 490 years – into three significant periods: 49 years, 434 years, and 7 years.[28]

The Coming of Messiah

Know therefore and understand, that from the going forth of the commandment to restore and to build Jerusalem unto the Messiah the Prince shall be seven weeks, and threescore and two weeks: the street shall be built again, and the wall, even in troublous times.

(Dan. 9:25)[29]

Seven weeks + sixty-two weeks = sixty-nine weeks of seven years—483 years. Here is my paraphrase of this verse: "Daniel, God wants you to know that from the time that the commandment is given to restore and rebuild Jerusalem until the coming of the Messiah will be 483 years." Artaxerxes gave that decree to Nehemiah in 445 BC (Neh. 2:1-8), and 483 years from that date would be the year AD 32. That was the year Jesus rode into Jerusalem on a donkey, presenting Himself to be Israel's Messiah (Zech. 9:9; Matt. 21:1-9). On that first Palm Sunday, people

THE TIME OF THE END

cut down branches from trees and laid them, along with garments, on the path as Jesus approached riding on the donkey. And as they did they shouted, "Hosanna to the Son of David! Blessed is He that cometh in the name of the Lord! Hosanna in the highest!

The Prophecy That the Messiah Would Be Killed

Notice that the prophecy states that after the Messiah appeared, He would be "cut off." The Hebrew word *karath* means to destroy, or kill. The Scofield Reference Bible tells us the words "not for himself" should be translated, "have nothing"—that is nothing of the regal glory that was rightly His.

> And after threescore and two weeks shall Messiah be cut off, but not for himself: and the people of the prince that shall come shall destroy the city and the sanctuary; and the end thereof shall be with a flood, and unto the end of the war desolations are determined.
>
> (Dan. 9:26)

Next, notice that after Messiah's death, God told Daniel the city of Jerusalem would be destroyed, including the Jewish temple. Jesus was crucified in AD 32 and then a few years later Titus and his Roman Legions came and destroyed the city, destroyed the temple, and drove the Jews out of their land. That was the "flood" or deluge mentioned here. The Jews were a people without a country from AD 70 until 1948 when they were allowed to return to the land of Israel. Isn't the Word of God amazing? This prophecy was given to Daniel in 538 BC. It was given over 500 years before the events it speaks of occurred.

The Seventieth Week

In verse 26 we see the temple destroyed, but notice in verse 27 the temple is back. See the words "sacrifice" and "oblation"? This refers to the animal sacrifices and grain offerings in the temple. When there is not a temple in Jerusalem, there is neither a sacrifice nor an oblation.

This can only mean one thing: the events described in verse 27 are yet to come. There has not been a temple since AD 70. The seventieth week of Daniel is still future.

There is, therefore, a *gap* between verses 26 and 27 of approximately 2,000 years. But why? After the Jewish nation rejected the Messiah, and had Him crucified on a Roman cross, God stopped using the Jew to represent Him on earth. He set Israel aside and started a new thing called "the church." The church is composed of all true believers in Jesus Christ, Jew and Gentile. All true believers are indwelt with the Spirit of God. The church started on the day of Pentecost (Acts 2). The church is described in 1 Corinthians 12:12-14, and Ephesians 3:1-12.

For the past 2,000 years God has used the church, not Israel, to represent Him on earth. Christ will one day come in the sky, and call His church up. At that moment all true believers in Jesus Christ will join Him in the air, and He will take them to heaven (1 Thess. 4:13-17). When the church has gone to heaven, God will then focus once again, on Israel. That brings us to Daniel's seventieth week.

> And he shall confirm the covenant with many for one week: and in the midst of the week he shall cause the sacrifice and the oblation to cease, and for the overspreading of abominations he shall make it desolate, even until the consummation, and that determined shall be poured upon the desolate.
>
> (Dan. 9:27)

Who is "he" in this verse? "He" is the Roman "prince that *shall come*" (v. 26). Once again, God speaks about the coming Antichrist. Since Israel became a nation again in 1948 there are two things that the Jews have wanted but have not been able to obtain. First, they want peace. They live under the constant threat of war. The Muslims have vowed to wipe Israel off the map. Second, they want to rebuild their temple that was destroyed by the Romans in AD 70, but they can't. The Muslims won't allow it because that temple site is "holy ground" for them.

The Roman prince (the Antichrist) will enter into a peace agreement with Israel. We think he will not only guarantee peace, but will also allow Israel to rebuild the temple. Notice the peace agreement will be for "one week." That is the final week, the seventieth week, the final seven years before Christ returns to earth. It is called the tribulation period. Notice what the Roman prince will do in the middle of the week (after three-and-a-half years). He will break his covenant. The Jews will be forbidden to sacrifice in their temple. Instead, he will demand that everybody worship him. The apostle Paul said the Antichrist will go to the temple and sit, "showing himself that he is God" (2 Thess. 2:1-9). The last three-and-a-half years of that final "week" will be a nightmare for the people of earth.

But by that time multitudes of people will have come to faith in the Messiah—Jesus. The believers who escape the onslaught of the Antichrist will be looking for Christ to come and set up His kingdom (Matt. 24:15-31; Dan. 8:25; Zech. 13:8-9, 14-21; Rev. 7:9-14, 19:11-12).

The cause of all the wars, all the sins, and all the confusion in our world is Satan, the enemy of God. Rejecting Jesus Christ always brings disaster, and our world, for the most part, has rejected Him. Following Christ brings joy, direction, peace, and fulfillment in one's life. Aren't you glad you are following Him?

Questions for Discussion
or Personal Study Emphasis

1. How long has it been since there has been a temple in Jerusalem?

2. Why was the temple destroyed?

3. After nearly 1,900 years in exile, the Jews once again have a nation, Israel. In your opinion what is the significance of the Jews being back in their land?

4. Will there ever be another temple in Jerusalem?

5. Whom did God use in the Old Testament to represent Him here on earth? Whom has God used to represent Him since the time of the resurrection of Christ? Whom will God use to represent Him during the final "week" (seven years) of Daniel?

6. Why is there a gap of roughly 2,000 years between Daniel 9:26 and 9:27?

7. Where does it say in the Old Testament that the Messiah would be killed?

Chapter Thirteen

THE INVISIBLE WAR

Daniel Chapter 10

All of the facts contained in the Bible are important. If they were not important, God would not have put them there. In Daniel chapter 10, we learn about a war that is unlike any war ever fought in human history. It is a war not fought against flesh and blood, but against the spiritual forces of wickedness (Eph. 6:12). It is an invisible war. We cannot see the battles, or the participants, and we cannot hear the sounds of battle, but they are very real, nevertheless.

When Lucifer, the angel, rebelled against God, one third of all the angels in heaven followed him. These fallen angels are called demons, and Lucifer, their leader, is called "Satan" or "the devil." Satan organized these fallen spirits into an army. His goal is to keep people from knowing and worshipping the true God. His ultimate goal is to get the people of earth to worship him, and him only.

These invisible spiritual forces are busy doing their evil work everywhere in our world. Their enemies are the good angels, the gospel of Jesus Christ, and the prayers of God's people, the believers. Friend, God wants you to know about this ongoing, invisible spiritual war. This war is going on right now all around us, and in the space above us.

The Burden of Daniel—Verses 1-3

Liberals attack this chapter beginning with the opening lines. They say, "It says here it was in the third year of Cyrus, but Daniel 1:21 says Daniel only continued until the first year of Cyrus." There is, however, no discrepancy here. In 1:21 Daniel tells us when he retired from his government career. In 10:1 he tells us he was still alive and active two years later. The year was 536 BC, and Daniel was then approximately eighty-five years of age.

> In the third year of Cyrus king of Persia a thing was revealed unto Daniel, whose name was called Belteshazzar; and the thing was true, but the time appointed was long: and he understood the thing, and had understanding of the vision.
>
> (Dan. 10:1)

This verse is difficult because it seems to convey the following truths: the Jewish people would have great trouble for a long time. They were to experience war and much suffering. Comments by John Walvoord and Warren Wiersbe follow.

> The Hebrew here, *saba gadol,* has been variously translated "great warfare," "a great task" or, more freely, "involved great suffering." The implication is that this period involves great conflict and trouble for the people of God.[30]

> The vision God showed him was true, and Daniel understood the message of the vision and realized that it would be fulfilled many years later. The phrase "the time appointed was long" can also be translated "and of great conflict". Daniel would learn that his people would experience great suffering in the years ahead, but that the Lord would watch over them and ultimately establish the promised kingdom.[31]

A short time earlier (one to two years), 50,000 Jewish captives in Babylon were allowed to return to Jerusalem to rebuild the temple, but their enemies forced them to stop their efforts (Ezra 4:1-5, 24). The news traveled slowly in those days, but it finally came to Daniel's attention that the work on the temple had stopped and his fellow Jews were suffering amidst the ruins of Jerusalem. The text indicates Daniel was burdened for his nation. We can understand that, can't we? I, too, am burdened for our nation and you are too, aren't you? If America doesn't repent of her sins, the day will come when the people of this land will suffer badly, and say, "I never thought it would come to this."

> In those days I, Daniel, was mourning three full weeks. I ate no pleasant bread, neither came flesh nor wine in my mouth, neither did I anoint myself at all, till three whole weeks were fulfilled.
>
> (Dan. 10:2-3)

The Vision of Daniel

Throughout this book Daniel documented dates and places. The real author of Scripture is the Holy Spirit of God, and He was directing Daniel's thoughts as he wrote.

> And in the four and twentieth day of the first month, as I was by the side of the great river, which is Hiddekel.
>
> (Dan. 10:4)

Daniel's last prophetic vision begins in verse five, and it extends all the way to the end of the book. As his vision began that day, he saw an awesome sight of a man, but it was no ordinary man. There is room for other views, but I believe that Daniel saw the God-man, Jesus Christ. Compare John's description of the glorified Christ (Rev. 1:13-18) with Daniel's vision and you will see the similarities.

> Then I lifted up mine eyes, and looked, and behold, a certain man clothed in linen, whose loins were girded with fine gold of Uphaz:

153

his body also was like the beryl, and his face as the appearance of lightning, and his eyes as lamps of fire, and his arms and his feet like in colour to polished brass, and the voice of his words like the voice of a multitude.

(Dan. 10:5-6)

Those who were there with Daniel that day didn't see anything. They sensed the divine presence, and they hid themselves. Have you ever wondered what the lost people of earth will think when Christ appears in the sky to take the believers (His church) to heaven before the tribulation begins? Well, they won't see anything. They won't see Christ in the sky, and they won't see the believers rise to meet Him. This great coming event known as the rapture will be over "in a moment, in the twinkling of an eye" (1 Cor. 15:51). Try this: focus your eyes on something, then blink. That's how fast Christ will snatch up His church. Isn't our Lord's power incredible! One "blink" and we'll be gone!

And I Daniel alone saw the vision: for the men that were with me saw not the vision; but a great quaking fell upon them, so that they fled to hide themselves.

(Dan. 10:7)

Daniel was overwhelmed with the vision, and no wonder, for mortal man is always overwhelmed in the presence of Deity. There are examples all through the Bible of this. Our day is not the day for visions. I have never seen Christ, but there have been a few special times when in prayer, He was so close I was overwhelmed with His presence. When He draws near, we are keenly aware of our sinfulness, and our tears flow like rain. It is a humbling experience. It is a life-changing experience. I wish for you this indescribable experience.

Therefore I was left alone, and saw this great vision, and there remained no strength in me: for my comeliness was turned in me into corruption, and I retained no strength. Yet heard I the voice of his words: and when I heard the voice of his words, then was I in a deep sleep on my face, and my face toward the ground.

(Dan. 10:8-9)

The Message to Daniel

Suddenly an angel appeared and touched Daniel and brought him to his hands and knees. Then the angel comforted him with a few kind words and ordered him to stand. A trembling Daniel stood to his feet, and then the angel informed him he had been in an invisible war for three weeks.

> And, behold, an hand touched me, which set me upon my knees and upon the palms of my hands. And he said unto me, O Daniel, a man greatly beloved, understand the words that I speak unto thee, and stand upright: for unto thee am I now sent. And when he had spoken this word unto me, I stood trembling. Then said he unto me, Fear not, Daniel: for from the first day that thou didst set thine heart to understand, and to chasten thyself before thy God, thy words were heard, and I am come for thy words. But the prince of the kingdom of Persia withstood me one and twenty days: but, lo, Michael, one of the chief princes, came to help me; and I remained there with the kings of Persia.
>
> (Dan. 10:10-13)

Who was this prince? He could not have been a human. No human being could withstand a powerful angel. So who was this "prince of the kingdom of Persia?" He was an evil angel (demon) assigned by Satan to the kingdom of Persia. A good angel was sent by God to deliver a prophecy to Daniel, but this evil prince blocked him, and the two opposing forces fought for three weeks. Finally, another angel, Michael, came to help the good angel. But why did it take Michael three weeks to get there? My guess is that Michael had been fighting back other demons in another part of the world. The angel Michael, you know, is the protector of Israel, so he was probably involved in the spiritual battle going on at that same time in Jerusalem (Ezra 4).

Satan had a "prince" over the kingdom of Persia. Satan has a "prince" over every nation on earth. Did you know that Satan has a prince over the United States of America? These "prince" demons are constantly influencing national leaders to move further and further away from God. They influence national leaders to go to war. Their wicked influence always brings death and destruction. They influence people to become wicked and immoral. Because of their influence, people and nations turn away from God. That is why prayer is so important. Wiersbe said, "But when we pray, God directs the armies of Heaven to fight on our behalf, even though we know nothing about the battles that are being waged in this invisible war (see 2 Kings 6:17)."[32]

Having explained the three-week delay in his coming, the angel proceeded to tell Daniel the *purpose* of his coming. He had come to tell Daniel what would happen to his people (the Jews, Israel) in the "latter days." The term "latter days" refers to the time of trouble that is still to come in Israel (the tribulation). At the end of that time of trouble the Messiah will come to the rescue of the Jews, put an end to the wars on earth, and will then establish His earthly kingdom in Jerusalem.

> Now I am come to make thee understand what shall befall thy people in the latter days: for yet the vision is for many days.
>
> (Dan. 10:14)

In the presence of this powerful messenger of God, Daniel once again lost his strength. He couldn't even speak, so the heavenly messenger touched him and strengthened him once again.

> And when he had spoken such words unto me, I set my face toward the ground, and I became dumb. And, behold, one like the similitude of the sons of men touched my lips: then I opened my mouth, and spake, and said unto him that stood before me, O my lord, by the vision my sorrows are turned upon me, and I have retained no strength.

For how can the servant of this my lord talk with this my lord? for as for me, straightway there remained no strength in me, neither is there breath left in me. Then there came again and touched me one like the appearance of a man, and he strengthened me, and said, O man greatly beloved, fear not: peace be unto thee, be strong, yea, be strong. And when he had spoken unto me, I was strengthened, and said, Let my lord speak; for thou hast strengthened me.

(Dan. 10:15-19)

Finally the angel informed Daniel that he would once again fight against the evil angel known as the Prince of Persia, and later against another evil angel, the Prince of Greece. You know what this shows us? It shows us there is constant warfare in spiritual victory.

Then said he, Knowest thou wherefore I come unto thee? and now will I return to fight with the prince of Persia: and when I am gone forth, lo, the prince of Grecia shall come. But I will shew thee that which is noted in the scripture of truth: and there is none that holdeth with me in these things, but Michael your prince.

(Dan. 10:20-21)

Wiersbe believes the unnamed angel in this chapter is Gabriel and commented as follows:

Finally, the angel made it clear that the battle wasn't yet over. As soon as he finished instructing Daniel, Gabriel would return to assist Michael in battling the prince of Persia and the prince of Greece, two satanic evil angels who were opposing the plans of the Lord for these nations. The ruler of Persia had shown great kindness and mercy to the Jews in allowing them to return home, and Satan was against this decision. God also had plans for Greece (11:2-4) and Satan wanted to interfere there. One reason why God commands His people to pray for those in authority is so that God's will, not Satan's plans, might be fulfilled in their lives (1 Tim. 2:1-3). The destiny of more than one nation has been changed because God's people have fervently prayed. "For the weapons of our warfare are not carnal but mighty in God for pulling down strongholds, casting down arguments and every high thing that exalts itself against the knowledge of God, bring every thought into captivity to the obedience of Christ."

(2 Cor. 10:4-5 NKJV)[33]

God wants us to know that there is an ongoing, invisible spiritual war where evil fallen angels fight against the good and faithful angels. This war is going on right now all around us, and in the space above us. That is why we need to pray, and witness to the lost, and live lives that glorify not self, but God. That is our part in the spiritual war. Are you involved in this warfare or are you merely watching from the sidelines? Friend, I want to encourage you to commit yourself freely to the God who saved you. I want to remind you we have "only one life, and it'll soon be past, only what's done for Christ will last

Questions for Discussion or Personal Study Emphasis

1. The text tells us that Daniel was overwhelmed with the vision. Discuss why. Discuss similar examples in both the Old Testament and the New Testament.

2. Discuss current events both in our nation and internationally in view of the "invisible war." What do you see the unseen forces of evil doing?

3. What are Satan's goals?

4. Will Satan accomplish his goals?

5. What weapons do believers in Christ have for use against the unseen enemies of our times?

6. Discuss 1 John 5:19.

7. Memorize Ephesians 6:12.

Chapter Fourteen

WAR, WARS AND STILL MORE WARS TO COME

Daniel 11:1-35

The prophecies of this chapter deal with war after war in the Middle East. We know from secular history that all of the wars prophesied, with the exception of those that will occur during the "time of the end," did indeed take place.

For thousands of years nations have risen up against other nations and men have had to go to war. Time after time, after time, battlefields have been strewn with the lifeless bodies of young soldiers, and the earth has been stained with their blood. The sacrifice of human lives however, means nothing to wicked rulers. In this chapter we will see tyrants rise and fall and we will see that process take place over and over again.

Historically, the bullies of this world have been so filled with greed and lust for power that they lose their ability to think about the really important things such as God, eternity, heaven and hell. These despots are driven by a longing desire for "more." They always want more people to rule over, more riches, more power, more adoration and more recognition. Most despots are narcissists, and narcissists crave these things.

They tend to deceive themselves with grandiose dreams of invincibility. The simple indisputable fact, however, is every leader who rises to power will soon come to his end. The years of a leader's power and rule are just a tiny speck, on the time line of human history.

> For what is your life? It is even a vapor that appears for a little time, and then vanishes away.
>
> (James 4:14)

Prophecies That Have Already Been Fulfilled

The angel who appeared to Daniel in chapter 10 is still speaking as chapter 11 opens. Both the angel from heaven, and Daniel the aged prophet, had divine assignments to fulfill that day. The angel's assignment was to deliver all of the prophecies to Daniel. The angel does all of the speaking in this chapter. Daniel's assignment was to write down the prophecies word for word as the angel gave them to him.

The prophecies in this chapter concerning Gentile nations contain key events that relate to the nation Israel. The first set of prophecies that the angel spoke were fulfilled after Daniel's time on earth and are now ancient history. These are the ones we will discuss in this chapter.

Persia in Prophecy—Verses 1-2

> Also I, in the first year of Darius the Mede, even I, stood to confirm and to strengthen him.
>
> (Dan. 11:1)

Why did the angel have to help Darius in his first year as king? What was going on in Babylon that first year? It was one of those invisible, spiritual struggles that involved the Jews who were still being held captive in Babylon. The bad angels wanted Daniel and the rest of the Jews destroyed, but God worked it out so the Jews would have favor with the Medes and Persians, and soon they would be headed home to Israel. Walvoord commented as follows.

The opening verse of chapter 11 is often considered the closing verse of chapter 10. In it, the angel, seen in 10:18, declared his support to confirm and strengthen Darius the Mede from the very beginning of his reign in Babylon. The statement that the angel "stood" in verse 1 is probably used in *sensu bellico s. militari,* that is, standing as in a military conflict against the enemy as in 10:13. The ESV understands the angel's stand as in support of Darius, but it is possible that "him" refers not to Darius—for the angel must fight *against* the prince of Persia (10:13)—but to Michael, the prince of Israel, on whose side he contends (10:21). In this view the verse would mean that in Darius's first year, when the world power passed from the Babylonian kingdom to Medo-Persia, the angel stood by Michael, the guardian of Israel, until he succeeded in turning the new kingdom from hostility to favor toward Israel. The story of chapter 6 demonstrates that efforts were made in the first year of Darius to make him hostile toward Israel. But God sent His angel and shut the lions' mouths (Dan. 6:22). The miraculous deliverance by the angel caused Darius the Mede to reverse his policies to favor Israel (6:24-27). The beginning of the second great empire with the fall of Babylon in chapter 5 was, then, more than a military conquest or triumph of the armies of the Medes and Persians. It was a new chapter in the divine drama of angelic warfare behind the scenes, and the change was by divine appointment. [34]

Stephen Miller had this to say about this spiritual battle that took place in the first year of the reign of Darius.

In 11:1 Gabriel related that he had helped Michael in some manner "in the first year of Darius the Mede" (ca. 538 B.C., two years before this vision). Since Michael (Israel's prince) was involved, the conflict must have concerned the Jewish people. The text does not name the occasion of this particular struggle, but it probably involved Cyrus's decree to allow the Jews to return to Palestine. Cyrus released the Jews, but unknown to the Persian monarch angelic forces played a part in that decision.[35]

And now will I shew thee the truth. Behold, there shall stand up yet three kings in Persia; and the fourth shall be far richer than they all: and by his strength through his riches he shall stir up all against the realm of Grecia.

(Dan. 11:2)

The fourth king after the rule of Darius we know from history was Xerxes I. His vast empire stretched from Ethiopia to India. But it wasn't enough; he wanted more. He used his great wealth to assemble an army of hundreds of thousands to invade Greece (480 BC), but he was defeated, and returned to Babylon. The Persian Empire would never recover from that costly defeat in Greece.

Greece in Prophecy—Verses 3-4

Thousands of young Greek soldiers died on the fields of battle, and from that point on the Greeks had a loathing hatred for the Persians. One hundred and thirty-two years later, the Greeks got even. Alexander the Great was on the move with his massive army conquering lands and people with lightning speed. The Persian Empire fell to Alexander (332 BC), and then his kingdom was divided among four of his generals, just as the angel in our text predicted. These prophecies were given to Daniel by the angel in 536 BC, over 200 years before they were fulfilled.

And a mighty king shall stand up, that shall rule with great dominion, and do according to his will. And when he shall stand up, his kingdom shall be broken, and shall be divided toward the four winds of heaven; and not to his posterity, nor according to his dominion which he ruled: for his kingdom shall be plucked up, even for others beside those.

(Dan. 11:3-4)

Wiersbe explained how God used these events later on to bring glory to Himself.

Once again, Alexander's incredible conquests were part of the sovereign plan of God. The spread of the Greek language and Greek culture assisted in the eventual spread of the gospel and the Greek New Testament. Alexander's goal was not just to conquer territory but to bring people together in a "united empire." His soldiers married women from the conquered nations, and Alexander's empire became a "melting pot" for all peoples. This too assisted in the spread of the gospel centuries later.[36]

Egypt and Syria in Prophecy—Verses 5-20

The prophecies in verses 5-20 focus on two of the four divisions of the Greek Empire after the death of Alexander, the Ptolemaic (Egyptian) and the Seleucus (Syrian). In these prophecies "the king of the south" refers to the Egyptian pharaoh, and "the king of the north" refers to the leader of Syria. The angel's prophecies focused on these two nations because the tiny nation of Israel lay between them, and the seemingly endless movement of troops from both directions through Israel created a hardship for the Jews. Several good conservative scholars have researched the kings mentioned in prophecy in these verses. Wiersbe is one of them.

Ptolemy I Soter and Seleucus I Nicator (v. 5). Seleucus was the stronger of the two and ruled over a large empire, but it was his alliance with Ptolemy that enabled him to seize the throne of Syria.

Ptolemy II Philadelphus and Antiochus II Theos (v. 6). As was often done in the days of monarchies, the rulers used marriage as a means of forming strong political alliances, a policy Solomon had followed (1 Kings 3:1, 11:1 ff.). However, Ptolemy demanded that Antiochus divorce his wife Laodice in order to marry his daughter Berenice. Ptolemy died after two years, so Seleucus took back his former wife, who then murdered both him and Berenice. It was one marriage where they all didn't live happily ever after. *"She will not retain her power, and he and his power will not last."*

(Dan. 11:6 NIV)

Ptolemy III Euergetes and Seleucus II Callinicus (vv. 7-9). The new king of Egypt was the brother of Berenice, and he was intent on defending his sister's honor and avenging her death. He attacked the northern power, won the victory, and collected a great deal of wealth. Then the two kings ignored each other for some years until Seleucus attacked Egypt in 240, was defeated, and had to return home in shame. He was killed by a fall from his horse, and his son Seleucus III Soter took the throne, only to be assassinated four years later. Antiochus III the Great, who ruled from 223 to 187, succeeded him.

Ptolemy IV Philopater and Antiochus III the Great (vv. 10-19). The sons of Seleucus II were Seleucus III, who was a successful general but was killed in battle and Antiochus III the Great, who carried out the Syrian military program with great skill. He regained lost territory from Egypt, but in 217 the Egyptian army defeated the Syrians. This didn't stop Antiochus, for he took his army east and got as far as India.

In 201, Antiochus mustered another large army, joined forces with Philip V of Macedon, and headed for Egypt (vv. 13-16), where he won a great victory against Ptolemy V Epiphanes. Contrary to God's law, but in fulfillment of the prophecies (visions), some of the Jews in Palestine joined with Antiochus, hoping to break free of Egyptian control; but their revolt was crushed (v. 14). Antiochus not only conquered Egypt and Sidon (v. 15), but also "the glorious land" of Palestine (v. 16).

Once again marriage enters the scene. Antiochus offered to negotiate with the Egyptian leaders and to marry his daughter Cleopatra I to Ptolemy V, who was seven years old at the time! He hoped that his daughter would undermine the Egyptian government from within and use her position to help him take over. However, Cleopatra was loyal to her husband, so the marriage stratagem didn't succeed.

Antiochus decided to attack Greece but was defeated at Thermopylae (191) and Magnesia (189). The "prince for his own behalf" (v. 18) was the Roman consul and general Lucius Cornelius Scipio Asiaticus, who led the Roman and Greek forces to victory over Antiochus. At an earlier meeting, Antiochus had insulted the Roman general, but the Romans had the last word. The Syrian leader died in 187, and his successor was his son Seleucus IV Philopator, who oppressed the Jewish people by raising taxes so he could pay tribute to Rome. Shortly after he sent his treasurer Heliodorus to plunder the Jewish temple, Seleucus Philopator suddenly dies (probably poisoned), thus fulfilling verse 20. This opened the way for the wicked Antiochus Epiphanies to seize the throne.

As you review the history of the relationship between Egypt and Syria, and the family relationships among the Seleucids, you can't help but realize that human nature hasn't changed over these thousands of years. The ancient world had its share of intrigue, political deception, violence, greed, and war. The lust for power and wealth drove men and women to violate human rights and break divine laws, to go to any length to get what they wanted. They slaughtered thousands of innocent people, plundered the helpless, and even killed their own relatives, just to wear a crown or sit on a throne.

While God is not responsible for the evil that men and women have done in the name of government and religion, He is still the Lord of history and continues to work out His plans for humankind. Studying the evil deeds of past rulers could make us cynical, but we must remember that one day *"the earth shall be filled with the knowledge of the glory of the Lord, as the waters cover the sea" (Hab. 2:14).* [35]

Antiochus Epiphanies in Prophecy—Verses 21-35

The next group of verses contains prophecies concerning the notorious Syrian king named Antiochus Epiphanes. Editor Stephen Miller's comments on these versus are helpful:

The historical information in verses 2-20 was furnished in order to introduce the Seleucid-Greek ruler, Antiochus IV Epiphanes

(175-163 B.C.) the "little horn" of chapter 8 (see Dan 8:9-12, 23-25). Much attention was given to this individual in the Book of Daniel because his actions profoundly affected Israel. The career of Antiochus may be divided as follows: accession to the throne and early reign (11:21-24), a further description of the first Egyptian war and subsequent Jewish persecution (11:25-28), the second Egyptian campaign (11:29-30A), and further persecutions of the Jews (11:30b-35).

Antiochus IV is labeled a "contemptible person (*"a despised person"*) by the Scripture writer because from the Jewish vantage point he was a monster. He persecuted the Jews, slaughtering thousands, and represented one of the greatest threats to the true religion in all of Israel's history. This arrogant monarch referred to himself as Epiphanes, the "Manifest One" or "Illustrious One"; but others called him Epimanes, the "Madman."

After his first Egyptian campaign (ca. 169 B.C.), Antiochus attacked Jerusalem ("holy covenant") and wreaked havoc on the Jewish people (v. 8). He massacred eighty thousand men, women, and children (2 Macc. 5:12-14) and then looted the Temple with the help of the evil high priest, Menelaus (see Macc. 5:15-21). In 168 B.C. Antiochus invaded Egypt again but this campaign did not turn out like the earlier one (v. 29). He encountered opposition from the "ships of the western coastlands [kittim]," that is, the Roman fleet that had come to Alexandria at the request of the Ptolemies (v. 30).

In 167 B.C. the suppression of the Jewish religion began on a grand scale (1 Macc. 1:41 ff.; 2 Macc. 6:1 ff.). Jewish religious practices such as circumcision, possessing the Scriptures, sacrifices, and fest days were forbidden on penalty of death (1 Macc. 1:50, 63). Desecration of the Jewish religion reached its climax in December 167 B.C. (1 Macc. 54) when an altar or idol-statue to Olympian Zeus (Jupiter) was erected in the Temple ("the abomination that causes desolation"), and ten days later sacrifices, probably including swine (see 1 Macc. 1:47; 2 Macc. 6:4-5), were offered on the altar (see 1 Macc. 1:54, 59).

Yet even in this dark period, there were true believers among the Jews who remained faithful to their God (v. 32; see 1 Macc. 1:62-63). Foremost among those who resisted the oppressive measures of Antiochus were the Maccabee, the family of a certain priest names Mattathias (1 Macc. 2:1ff.). He had five sons John, Simon, Judas, Eleazar, and Jonathan, three of whom (Judas, Jonathan, and Simon) became known as the Maccabees, although the term *Maccabeus* ("hammer") originally was given only to Judas (1 Macc. 2:4). The Maccabees overthrew the Syrian yoke through a series of brilliant military victories against Antiochus's military commanders, Apollonius, Seron, Gorgias and Lysias (1 Macc. 3:10-4:35) between 166 (or 165) and 164 B.C. and as a result the temple was rededicated to the Lord on December 14, 164 B.C. (1 Macc. 4:52). Verses 33-35 refer to true believers (*"wise"*) who would remain faithful in spite of persecution.

"A little help" (v. 34) is the Maccabean revolt that grew and eventually threw off the Syrian yoke. The purpose of Israel's fiery ordeal was to cleanse individuals and the nation as a whole of sinful practices and strengthen their faith. Antiochus IV died in 163 B.C. during an expedition in Persia (1 Macc. 6:1-6; 2 Macc. 9:1-29), bringing to an "end" both his wicked life and his atrocities against God's people.[38]

Take note of that phrase at the end of verse 31: "the abomination that makes desolate" because it is an important one. You have probably heard this phrase, yet you probably are not sure what it means. The word abomination in Hebrew means "a detestable thing" or "a detestable idol." The Hebrew word for desolate means "deserted." No Jew would worship in the temple after this wicked man had desecrated it for two reasons: one spiritual and one physical. First the temple was spiritually polluted, and second, the fear of physical death at the hand of Antiochus, the "Madman."

The Abomination That Makes Desolate in End-Time Prophecy

As we have already noted (chapter 8), Antiochus Epiphanes is a picture of the still-to-come Antichrist. The "abomination that maketh desolate" foretold by the angel to Daniel was fulfilled by Antiochus in 168 BC. The Bible states clearly that the coming Antichrist will also desecrate the Jewish temple. Although the Jews haven't had a temple in nearly 2,000 years (AD 70) they will have one soon. When the disciples asked Jesus what would be the sign of his coming and of the end of the age (Matt. 24:3) He told them they would see "the abomination of desolation stand in the holy place" (Matt. 24:15). Jesus said that as soon as they see this event take place they should quickly "flee into the mountains" (Matt. 24:16) because "great tribulation" would follow (Matt. 24:21). The apostle Paul also referred to this coming event by teaching that this "man of sin" would sit in the temple of God showing the world "that he is God" (2 Thess. 2:3-4). The apostle John informs us that the coming "beast" will blaspheme "against God . . . make war with the saints" and cause that "all that dwell upon the earth shall worship him." But his exalted time of great power shall only last forty-two months (see Rev. 13:4-8). Then our Lord will return to earth and "the beast" will be "cast alive into a lake of fire" (Rev. 19:20).

Every tyrant who rises to power becomes obsessed with his importance, and authority, but in a short time death comes. Death without Christ brings eternal suffering. Where are all the wicked rulers of history today? They are suffering in the fires of hell for their sins against God and humanity (Luke 16:22-24; John 3:36).

Questions for Discussion
or Personal Study Emphasis

1. Why have there been so many evil rulers in human history?

2. Do you see any evidence in any current events that would suggest there is an unseen spiritual battle in process in our world?

3. Tyrants often have a lot of power, but they tend to deceive themselves. Name and discuss some ways they deceive themselves.

4. Read Jeremiah 17:9 in several different translations and discuss.

5. What does the phrase "the abomination that makes desolate" mean?

6. How can the study of Bible prophecy strengthen the faith of Christians alive today? In what other ways can the study of prophecy help us?

7. How will Bible prophecy help the tribulation saints?

Chapter Fifteen

NO MORE WAR

Daniel 11:35-45

One day Jesus is coming back to this earth. When He comes He will straighten out all of man's problems. Until Jesus returns, however, there will continue to be crime, broken homes, sin of all kinds, and more wars. How horrible is war! War is nation against nation, one man against another man, kill or be killed.

On a cold, dark afternoon in February of 1945, after leaving the one-room country school that we attended, my big sister, big brother, and I were walking to our grandparents' home where we were staying. Our parents both worked in a war plant about twenty miles away. We didn't get to see them too often because travel was very difficult during those war years. Suddenly, a car pulled up beside us and stopped. It was our parents, and something was wrong. They had both been crying. We had never seen our parents cry before. Then they said, "We just got word from overseas that your Uncle Leroy was killed in Belgium." Then they sped off to Norwich to be with Leroy's parents, my other set of grandparents. My grandparents never got over the loss of Leroy, their youngest son.

There have been wars for thousands of years, and the wars are getting bigger. Around seventy million people were killed in World War

173

II. That was the deadliest military conflict in all of history. I am glad that our Lord is coming back. When He comes, the Bible tells us that He will stop the killings, He will stop the wars, and He will establish worldwide peace.

The Big Leap Forward

Earlier in this chapter we read that the angel gave prophecies that day to Daniel concerning Persia, Greece, Egypt, and Syria. Then the angel prophesied concerning a wicked king who would rise to power, persecute the Jews, and desecrate the temple in Jerusalem. That king, we know from history, was Antiochus Epiphanies. His reign of terror, the angel declared, would be a time of purging for the Jews. Then the angel told Daniel this purging would continue until "the time of the end" (v. 35).

The "time of the end" is still future. It begins when the coming antichrist breaks his covenant with Israel (Dan. 9:27, Matt. 24: 3-24) midway through the tribulation period. The angel prophesied about the placing of the "abomination that maketh desolate" (v. 31). That took place in 168 BC. Then the angel leaped forward in time and prophesied about the "time of the end" which doesn't begin until after the rapture of the church. I call this "the big leap forward." That is a period of around 2, 200 years. That is a big leap isn't it?

Dr. Walvoord comments:

In verse 35 the purging process is said to continue "to the time of the end." It is clear that the persecutions of Antiochus were not the time of the end, even though they foreshadowed it. The mention of "the end," however, serves as a transition. From verse 36 on, the prophecy leaps the intervening centuries to predict events related to the last generation prior to God's judgment of Gentile power and its rulers, prophecy that has yet to be fulfilled.[39]

The "Big Head" Described

The angel gave Daniel a description of the coming Antichrist. Check out what the angel said about him and you will conclude that he will be a "big head." The king in verse 36 is the future Antichrist. This arrogant, evil man will do anything he wants to do. No one will be able to hold him accountable. When he talks or makes a speech his favorite subject will be himself. Talk about a "big head"!

> And the king shall do according to his will; and he shall exalt himself, and magnify himself above every god, and shall speak marvelous things against the God of gods, and shall prosper till the indignation be accomplished: for that that is determined shall be done.
>
> (Dan. 11:36)

There are some things in the concluding verses of this book that are straightforward and are therefore not to difficult to understand. Other things in these verses are not so clear. The angel told Daniel they will not be clear until "the time of the end" (Dan. 12:8-9). Walvoord explained, "The primary purpose of the revelation was to inform those who would live in that time. The confirming interpretation of history and prophecy fulfilled would be necessary before the final prophecies could be understood."[40]

This coming world leader will be an atheist (v. 37), and he will be a narcissist for he will "magnify himself" (vv. 36-37). He will want the attention, the praise, and adoration of the world, yet he will be without compassion for people.

> Neither shall he regard the God of his fathers, nor the desire of women, nor regard any god: for he shall magnify himself above all. But in his estate shall he honour the God of forces: and a god whom his fathers knew not shall he honour with gold, and silver, and with precious stones, and pleasant things. Thus shall he do in the most strong holds with a strange god, whom he shall acknowledge and increase with

glory: and he shall cause them to rule over many, and shall divide the land for gain.

(Dan. 11:37-39)

His god will be the god of force, and of military power. Walvoord said:

> For this world ruler to acknowledge something as supreme while already claiming to be God clearly indicates that "the god of fortresses" is not a person but the power to make war, symbolized by the term *fortress*. Examining all other passages relating to the end time, it becomes evident that the final world ruler's sole confidence is in military power, personified as "the god of fortresses." In other words, he is a complete materialist in contrast to all previous religions and all previous men who claimed divine qualities. This is blasphemy to the ultimate, the exaltation of human power and attainment. He is Satan's masterpiece, a human being who is Satan's substitute for Jesus Christ, hence properly identified as the Antichrist.[41]

The Biggest War in History

Soon, however, the Antichrist's empire will begin to fall apart. (For additional details, study the book of Revelation.) Then the world will be faced with the biggest war in all of history. The Bible calls it Armageddon. I often refer to it as Armageddon: World War III. There has been some confusion on this subject. Theodore Epp explains:

> The confusion lies in the use of the word "battle" in Revelation 16:14 and other passages referring to Armageddon. The word should be translated "war." It is more than one battle; it is a series of battles, or a campaign. So the Battle of Armageddon is, in reality, a campaign or war which will extend over several years, and then reach a terrible climax. Once this truth about the word "battle" is seen, a great deal of confusion about Armageddon is resolved. The last great war will involve many nations and will end in the decisive, final battle at

Armageddon. The nations of the world will fight against God and His forces.[42]

Some of the kings and nations referred to here are not disclosed, but remember the saints who will be living on earth at "the time of the end" will know who they are when they read these verses. Here is what we do know: Satan's demons will gather the armies of the world to fight at Armageddon (Rev. 16: 13-16).

And at the time of the end shall the king of the south push at him: and the king of the north shall come against him like a whirlwind, with chariots, and with horsemen, and with many ships; and he shall enter into the countries, and shall overflow and pass over. He shall enter also into the glorious land, and many countries shall be overthrown: but these shall escape out of his hand, even Edom, and Moab, and the chief of the children of Ammon. He shall stretch forth his hand also upon the countries: and the land of Egypt shall not escape. But he shall have power over the treasures of gold and of silver, and over all the precious things of Egypt: and the Libyans and the Ethiopians shall be at his steps. But tidings out of the east and out of the north shall trouble him: therefore he shall go forth with great fury to destroy, and utterly to make away many. And he shall plant the tabernacles of his palace between the seas in the glorious holy mountain; yet he shall come to his end, and none shall help him.

(Dan. 11: 40-45)

The Biggest Event in History

The biggest event in history will be the return of Jesus Christ to earth to set up His 1,000-year kingdom. When Jesus comes, He will stop the killings, He will stop the wars, and He will "make all things new" (Rev. 21:5). When Jesus returns He will take control immediately. When the Antichrist meets Christ, it's all over!

Behold, the day of the LORD cometh, and thy spoil shall be divided in the midst of thee. For I will gather all nations against Jerusalem to battle; and the city shall be taken, and the houses rifled, and the women ravished; and half of the city shall go forth into captivity, and the residue of the people shall not be cut off from the city. Then shall the LORD go forth, and fight against those nations, as when he fought in the day of battle. And his feet shall stand in that day upon the mount of Olives, which is before Jerusalem on the east, and the mount of Olives shall cleave in the midst thereof toward the east and toward the west, and there shall be a very great valley; and half of the mountain shall remove toward the north, and half of it toward the south. And the LORD shall be king over all the earth: in that day shall there be one LORD, and his name one. And this shall be the plague wherewith the LORD will smite all the people that have fought against Jerusalem; Their flesh shall consume away while they stand upon their feet, and their eyes shall consume away in their holes, and their tongue shall consume away in their mouth. (Zech. 14:1-4, 9, 12)

Yes, things are getting dark in our world, but Christians remember the greatest, biggest, grandest event in all of history is coming! Our Lord, the one who died for our sins and rose again, is coming!!! And when He comes, He will make all things right! One of our Lord's titles in Scripture is the Prince of Peace. I wrote a poem with that title. Here it is:

The Prince of Peace
A long time ago in Bethlehem
came the Prince of Peace, the Son of Man.
The prophet foretelling that He would come,
Said a virgin woman would have a son.
Born in a manger, the virgin birth,
The Prince of Peace had come to this earth.
Without any sin He lived His life,
He offered men peace, but they chose strife.

No More War

When He offered men peace, they turned Him down.
They gave Him a cross, instead of a crown.
But the Prince of Peace was willing to die,
He did it for sinners like you and I.
It was there on the cross that He paid for our sin,
And "by faith" He forgives us and gives peace within.
This world is filled with darkness and sin,
But one day He's coming back again.
Look around you and you will see,
Trouble and pain and misery.
We've been a race of rebels from the very start,
Man cannot have peace when there's war within his heart.
The masses are stuck in the muck and the mire,
Sin is raging like an out of control fire!
The Prince of Peace is coming! We are running out of time,
The Prince of Peace is coming! I can see Him in my mind.
The world is getting darker. Great are the sins of man.
The Prince of Peace is coming! He told us of His plan.
When He returns there will be a place,
For every saved member of our race.
He will do away with wickedness,
Man will enter an age of rest.
"No more war? What will it be?"
Peace on earth from sea to sea.
When Jesus comes, all wars will cease,
For Jesus is the Prince of Peace.

Questions for Group Discussion
or Bible Study Emphasis

1. How often do you think about the end times?

2. Many people avoid thinking about the end times. Why do you think that is?

3. Can you think about any technological advancement that will aid in the Antichrist's rise to power?

4. The angel prophesied that the "purging" process of the Jews under the persecution of Antiochus would continue until "the time of the end." That was nearly 2, 200 years ago. Have the Jews suffered purging down through the centuries to our day? Discuss examples.

5. The Jews, however, despite all of the persecution over these centuries of time, still exist and today are back in the land. What is the significance of this?

6. How often do you think about the time of peace that is coming when Christ returns?

Chapter Sixteen

The Time of the End and the Events That Will Follow

Daniel Chapter 12

When Daniel was a teenager, perhaps sixteen years of age, he was forced to leave his home in Jerusalem and, along with many other Jews, was taken captive into Babylon, where he would spend the rest of his life. Daniel loved the Lord, but in pagan Babylon Satan would test Daniel's devotion to God time after time. Daniel, however, had decided early in his life that he would serve the Lord, no matter what. The Lord blessed Daniel all through his life, and the reason for that was obvious. He lived a life of obedience to God.

It always pays to serve God. God is not a respecter of persons (Acts 10:34; Col. 3:25). He will bless anybody who serves Him. When a person sets out to live for the all-powerful, all knowing, living God, He will bless that person. The loving God of heaven pours out His blessings upon those who serve Him. There are many great truths revealed in the book of Daniel, but none greater than this: it pays to serve God.

The Great Tribulation—Verse 1

As chapter 12 opens the angel is still speaking to Daniel about the time of the end, and the events that will follow. The angel tells Daniel that this coming time of trouble will be the worst time of trouble in all of human history. Michael, the angel assigned by God to protect the Jews, will be on the job in Israel when the time comes.

> And at that time shall Michael stand up, the great prince which standeth for the children of thy people: and there shall be a time of trouble, such as never was since there was a nation even to that same time: and at that time thy people shall be delivered, every one that shall be found written in the book.
>
> (Dan. 12:1)

The Resurrection of Israel—Verse 2

In the Bible there are two separate, distinct groups that God calls His people. The Old Testament tell us His people were the Jews, the nation Israel. Two thousand years ago, however, when the long-awaited Messiah finally came, Israel rejected Him and had Him crucified. God then set Israel aside and began a new thing called "the church." The church (universal) is composed of all those who have accepted Jesus Christ as their Savior. God, however, is not done with the nation of Israel. One day God will once again deal with His Old Testament people, Israel. We do not know when this day will come, but we do know how long the Lord will deal with the Jews before the nation of Israel turns to Him. His dealing with the Jews will last seven years. This important period of time is often referred to as "Daniel's final week" because of the prophecy given in Daniel 9:24-27. To deepen your knowledge on this subject it would be helpful to go back and review the 12th chapter of this book, which is entitled "The Prophecy of the Seventy Weeks."

Before God begins dealing with Israel once again in a major way, He will remove the church (all believers) from earth. The apostle Paul told us about that coming event.

> But I would not have you to be ignorant, brethren, concerning them which are asleep, that ye sorrow not, even as others which have no

184

hope. For if we believe that Jesus died and rose again, even so them also which sleep in Jesus will God bring with him. For this we say unto you by the word of the Lord, that we which are alive and remain unto the coming of the Lord shall not prevent them which are asleep. For the Lord himself shall descend from heaven with a shout, with the voice of the archangel, and with the trump of God: and the dead in Christ shall rise first: then we which are alive and remain shall be caught up together with them in the clouds, to meet the Lord in the air: and so shall we ever be with the Lord. (1 Thess. 4:13-17)

A careful study of these verses reveals this resurrection is only for the New Testament church. The saints of the Old Testament are not resurrected at this time. Notice the souls the Lord brings with Him are those "who sleep in Jesus" (v. 16). Israel and the church represent two separate entities, two distinct dispensations, and they are further distinguished by two separate resurrections. The resurrection of the Old Testament saints will take place at the conclusion of "the time of the end" (the great tribulation) when Christ returns to earth. Verse two of our text speaks about the coming resurrection of the Old Testament saints and the saints who will be martyred in the great tribulation.

And many of them that sleep in the dust of the earth shall awake, some to everlasting life, and some to shame and everlasting contempt.
(Dan. 12:2)

"Many" refers to the believers who will be resurrected to everlasting life. The resurrection of the unbelievers to "everlasting contempt" will occur after the 1,000-year-rule of Christ (Rev. 20:4-15). Walvoord's research is helpful in understanding the 1,000-year "gap" between the two resurrections found in verse 2.

Some help is afforded in understanding Daniel 12:2 by appealing to more accurate translations. Actually the Hebrew seems to separate sharply the two classes of resurrection. Tregelles following earlier Jewish commentators translated verse 2, "And many from among the sleepers of the dust of the earth shall awake; these shall be unto everlasting life; but those the rest of the sleepers, those who do not awake at this time, shall be unto shame and everlasting contempt." Culver defends this translation by finding support in commentaries by Seiss, and West.[43]

Rewards and the Coming Millennium

And they that be wise shall shine as the brightness of the firmament; and they that turn many to righteousness as the stars for ever and ever.

(Dan. 12:3)

After the church has been raptured and taken to heaven by our Lord, many Jews will experience a spiritual "awakening" and will then zealously proclaim the gospel to the people of earth. Many Jews will be martyred for the faith during the tribulation. But when Christ returns to earth and stops the wars, these Jews will be resurrected and will "shine . . . forever and ever." We are not told what this shining will entail, but it will be a reward from God for the Jewish soul winners of the tribulation.

The Time of the End—Verses 4-10

What did the angel mean when he said to Daniel, "Seal the book"? Wiersbe commented:

The book was to be treasured and protected and shared with the Jewish people. However, the book was "sealed" in this sense: The full meaning of what Daniel wrote would not be understood until "the time of the end" (see Matt. 24:15). Even Daniel didn't fully understand all that he saw, heard, and wrote!

(Dan. 12:8)[44]

The term "the time of the end" or it's equivalent "in the end," appears repeatedly in this book (Dan. 8:17-19, 9:26, 11:35, 40, 45 and 12:4, 6, 9). The time of the end is the end of the age, not the end of the world. It will last three and a half years. This subject is covered in the introduction of this book. It may be helpful at this point to review what is written there. Wiersbe explains the last part of verse 4 as follows:

> "Many shall run to and fro, and knowledge shall be increased" is not a reference to automobiles and jet planes or the advancement of education. It has reference to the study of God's Word, in the last days, especially the study of prophecy. Amos 8:11-12 warns us that the day will come when there will be a famine of God's Word, and people will run here and there seeking for truth but won't find it. But God's promise to Daniel is that, in the last days, His people can increase in their knowledge of prophetic Scripture as they apply themselves to the Word of God. Some interpret "to and fro" to mean running one's eyes to and fro over the pages of Scripture.[45]

Next, Daniel saw two angels on the banks of the Tigris River and he saw Christ in a pre-incarnate form in the air above the river. Compare Daniel's previous description of Christ in chapter 10, verses 5 and 6. Before Christ ascended into heaven, Luke tells us He took His disciples up the Mount of Olives and there He lifted up His hands and blessed them (Luke 24:50). Daniel also saw Him lift both hands.

> Then I Daniel looked, and, behold, there stood other two, the one on this side of the bank of the river, and the other on that side of the bank of the river. And one said to the man clothed in linen, which was upon the waters of the river, How long shall it be to the end of these wonders? And I heard the man clothed in linen, which was upon the waters of the river, when he held up his right hand and his left hand unto heaven, and sware by him that liveth forever that it shall be for a time, times, and an half; and when he shall have accomplished to scatter the power of the holy people, all these things shall be finished.
> (Dan. 12:5-7)

The expression *time* is a single unit. Times is a simple multiple unit (two). One-half is a half unit. Christ's answer to Daniel's question concerning the "time of the end" (vv. 1, 6), we believe, after comparing scripture with scripture was three and one-half years. This will be a time of terrible persecution of Israel.

Daniel heard but did not understand much of what he heard, so he asked for understanding. Daniel was then told the details of this prophecy concerning this coming time of tribulation for Israel are "sealed until the time of the end" (the last three and a half years of the seventieth "week"). (See Daniel 9:27.)

> And I heard, but I understood not: then said I, O my Lord, what shall be the end of these things? And he said, Go thy way, Daniel: for the words are closed up and sealed till the time of the end.
>
> (Dan. 12:8-9)

It will be a horrible time for the land of Israel. This coming time of persecution, however, will do what persecution has always done to believers. It will purify them.

> Many shall be purified, and made white, and tried; but the wicked shall do wickedly: and none of the wicked shall understand; but the wise shall understand.
>
> (Dan. 12:10)

Daniel was then informed there would be an additional seventy-five days extending beyond the three-and-one-half years of tribulation. He did not understand what would take place during these seventy-five days, but he, nevertheless, wrote down what he had been told.

> And from the time that the daily sacrifice shall be taken away, and the abomination that maketh desolate set up, there shall be a thousand two hundred and ninety days. Blessed is he that waiteth, and cometh to the thousand three hundred and five and thirty days.
>
> (Dan. 12:11-12)

THE TIME OF THE END AND THE EVENTS
THAT WILL FOLLOW

In Old Testament times a Jewish month was thirty days. Three and one-half years was, therefore, 1260 days. Verse 7 tells us that after the 1,200 days "all these things should be finished" (the great tribulation). So what are the extra thirty days in verse 11 and the extra forty-five days in verse 12? Since we are not told, we can only guess. When Christ returns and destroys the armies that are at war in and around Israel, the great tribulation of three-and-one-half years will end. But, before He sets up His kingdom here on earth, certain things will happen.

Before His kingdom is set up, Christ will judge the nations. No unbeliever will be allowed to enter Christ's kingdom. You can read about our Lord judging the nations in Matthew 25:31-46.

There will also be a judgment of the Jews. Our Lord will gather all Jews from the various nations of the world and then He will judge them.

> The significance of the 1,290 days and the 1,335 days isn't made clear, but there is a blessing attached to the second number. The starting point is the middle of the tribulation, when the abomination of desolation is set up in the temple. Since there are 1,260 days (three and a half years) before the tribulation ends, the 1,290 days would take us 30 days beyond the return of the Lord, and the 1,335 days 75 days beyond the end of the tribulation. We aren't told why these days are important or how they will be used to bring blessing to God's people. Certainly there are activities that the Lord must direct and tasks to accomplish, all of which will take time. Perhaps the greatest task is the regathering of His people from the nations of the world (Ezek. 20:33; Isa. 1:24-2:5, 4:2-6, 11:1-16), their purging, and their preparation to enter the promised kingdom.[46]

Those who have rejected Christ will not be allowed in His kingdom. Unbelievers will hear these words from Jesus Christ, earth's new king: "Depart from me ye cursed into everlasting fire, prepared for the devil and his angels" (Matt. 25:34).

However, earth's new King shall welcome the believers into the kingdom (Matt. 25:34). These are the "blessed" that we read about in Daniel 12:12.

> Blessed is he who waits, and comes to the one thousand three hundred and thirty-five days.
>
> (Dan. 12:12)

What a life Daniel had. He decided early in life to serve the Lord, thus the Lord blessed him. Daniel was used of God in great ways. He even stood before powerful kings. Daniel's story is one of many stories that teach us this great truth: It pays to serve God! Whatever we give up to serve the Lord is nothing compared to the blessings we receive for serving Him. Don't be afraid to give yourself totally to His service. Dedicate yourself to His service and soon He will send great blessings into your life. You will say, "It's true! Since I gave Him control of my life He has blessed me beyond measure! I wouldn't go back to where I was for anything!"

Daniel was now an old man. He had served the Lord all of his life. The angel has just one more thing to say to Daniel, and then Daniel would be free to go. He'd be able to rest a while, and then his body would die and his soul would suddenly be in heaven. The angel, however, reminded Daniel that he would one day stand upon this earth once again—when Christ comes!

> But go thou thy way till the end be: for thou shalt rest, and stand in thy lot at the end of the days.
>
> (Dan. 12:13)

Daniel was blessed in this life, he is blessed today in heaven, and he will be blessed in Christ's kingdom that is coming soon to this earth. All of us who have accepted Jesus as our Savior will also be here on earth during the kingdom age. Things are looking very bad on the world stage, and the Bible declares that things will get worse. Then Christ will come with all the saints from heaven and set up His kingdom. All of us who have accepted Him will live with Him on this earth! Our Lord is coming soon to this sin-darkened world, and He will make all things right. Aren't you glad? In the meantime, serve Him, and He will bless your life.

How to Be Sure You Are Going to Heaven

Religion cannot save us, and we cannot save ourselves by doing "good works." The only way anyone can be saved is through faith in Jesus Christ. Every one of us must choose to accept Him or choose to reject Him. Here are four important spiritual truths:

1. **All of us are sinners**—"As it is written, There is none righteous, no, not one" (Rom. 3:10). "For all have sinned, and come short of the glory of God" (Rom. 3:23).

2. **Sin separates us from God**—"For the wages of sin is death" (Rom. 6:23). That is spiritual separation from God. Until our sin problem is taken care of by Christ, we can't *know* God. We can know there is a God, but we cannot *know* God.

3. **God loves you and wants you to have everlasting life**—"for God so loved the world that he gave his only begotten Son, that whosoever believeth in him should not perish, but have everlasting life" (John 3:16).

4. **Christ died in our place**—"But God commendeth his love toward us, in that, while we were yet sinners, Christ died for us" (Rom. 5:8).

Hell is a very real place. Jesus said it is a place where "the fire never shall be quenched" (Mark 9:43). Christ had you in mind when He hung on the cross. He paid the total price for your sins so you could be saved from eternal punishment and go to heaven when you die.

Christ rose from the dead.

"Christ died for our sins . . . He was buried . . . He rose again the third day according to the scriptures . . . He was seen of Cephas, then of the twelve. After that He was seen of above five hundred brethren at once" (1 Cor. 15:3-6).

Christ will give you everlasting life if you will come to Him by faith.

"That if thou shalt confess with thy mouth the Lord Jesus, and shalt believe in thine heart that God hath raised him from the dead, thou shalt be saved. For with the heart man believeth unto righteousness; and with the mouth confession is made unto salvation" (Rom. 10:9-10). "For whosoever shall call upon the name of the Lord shall be saved" (Rom. 10:13).

Christ loves you and will give you everlasting life if you will come to Him by faith. The choice is up to you. If you want to come to Christ by faith, you can do it with the following prayer:

Christ, I agree with you that I am a sinner. I do not want to die in my sins. The Bible says You loved me, You died for my sins on the cross, and You will save me if I would come to You by faith. I am doing that right now. Thank You for loving me, thank You for dying for my sins, and thank You for saving my soul. Amen.

"Now that I have accepted Christ, what other things should I do?"

God wants you to experience Him on a daily basis. He wants to have fellowship with you. In order for you to experience Him daily you should do the following:

1. **Read some Scripture from the Bible every morning** (Acts 17:11, Ps. 119:11). Start with the gospel of John.

2. **Pray** (John 15:7). After you have read some Scripture, spend a few minutes in prayer. First, confess your sin. We still sin after we are saved (1 John 1:8). When you sin after you are saved, you do not lose your salvation, because that was a gift from God (Rom. 6:23; Eph. 2:8-9). All who Christ saves will never perish (John 10:28). Fellowship with God, however, is fragile. He is a holy God, and we cannot have fellowship with Him unless we confess our sins. When we confess our sins to our heavenly Father, He forgives us and restores us to fellowship (1 John 1:5-9). Then, ask Him to help you live right throughout the day.

3. **Worship in a Bible-believing and teaching church weekly.** God tells us we should not forsake "the assembling of our selves together" (Heb. 10:25). If you start attending a good Bible-believing and teaching church, you will grow quickly as a Christian, you will make many new friends, and you will please God.

4. **Fill out the decision form on the next page.** Mail it to me and I will send you some free, helpful resource material designed to help you in your walk with Christ. May God richly bless you as you follow Him. The mailing address is.

Dr. Don Manley
First Baptist Church of Oxford
P. O. Box 5
Oxford, FL 34484

My Decision

Dear Don,

I have read your book, *The Time of the End*, and I have this day come to Christ by faith. I believe He died for my sins on the cross, and He rose again the third day. I have today accepted Christ as my Savior. Please send me the free resource material that you offered.

Date: _____

Name: _____

Address and zip code: _____

_____

_____

ENDNOTES

Introduction

1. John F. Walvoord, *Daniel the Key to Prophetic Revelation* (Chicago: Moody Press, 2012), 34.
2. Theodore Epp, *The Times of the Gentiles* (Lincoln: Back to the Bible, 1969), 14-15.

Chapter One

3. Catherine Drinker Bowen, *Miracle at Philadelphia* (Boston: Little, Brown and Co., 1966), 125-127.
4. Warren W. Wiersbe, *Be Resolute: (Daniel) Determining to Go God's Direction* (Colorado Springs: David C. Cook, 2008), 19.
5. Hal Lindsey, *Daniel* (Murrieta: Oracle House Publishing, Inc.), CD1.

Chapter Two

6. Walvoord, 47.
7. Wiersbe, 22.
8. Ibid., 25.

Chapter Three

9. Sam Vaknin, *Malignant Self Love* (Lidlja Rangelovska, 1999-2008), 35.

Chapter Five

10. Lehman Strauss, *The Prophecies of Daniel* (Neptune: Loizeaux Brothers, Inc., 1969), 108.

Chapter Seven

11. Merill C. Tenney, ed., *The Zondervan Pictorial Encyclopedia of the Bible* (Grand Rapids: Zondervan Publishing House, 1975, 1976), vol. 1, 446.
12. Robert Koldewey, *The Excavations at Babylon,* Agnes S. Johns, trans. (Ann Arbor, MI: University of Michigan Library, 1914), 103-4, quoted in Walvoord,.147.
13. Wiersbe, 84.
14. Herodotus, *Histories* 1:190-91, quoted in Walvoord, 158-159.

Chapter Eight

15. Carl Friedrich Keil, *Biblical Commentary on the Book of Daniel,* M.G. Easton, trans. (Grand Rapids: Eerdmans, 1955), 216, quoted in Walvoord 173-174.
16. Keil, 216, Goldingay, John, *Daniel, Word Biblical Commentary,* eds. David A. Hubbard and Glen W. Barker (Word, 1989) 132; Archer, Gleason L., Jr., "Daniel," Expositor's Bible Commentary, vol.7., ed. Frank E. Gaebelein (Grand Rapids: Zondervan 1985), 81 quoted in Walvoord, 173.
17. Lindsey, CD 5.

Chapter Nine

18. Wiersbe, 106.

19. Ibid., 106.
20. Ronald E. Showers, *The Most High God* (West Collingswood: The friends of Israel Gospel Ministry, Inc., 1982), 75.
21. Walvoord, 194.

Chapter Ten

22. Wiersbe, 112.
23. Driver, Samuel Rolles, *The Book of Daniel*, The Cambridge Bible for School and Colleges (Cambridge: Cambridge University Press, 1900), quoted in Walvoord, 205.
24. Strauss, 218-219.

Chapter Eleven

25. Wiersbe, 109.
26. Dr. Mark G. Cambron in a lecture at Florida Bible College.

Chapter Twelve

27. Walvoord, 250.
28. Wiersbe, 139.
29. Scofield Reference Bible.

Chapter Thirteen

30. Cf. Young, *Daniel*, 223; Leupold, *Daniel*, 443; Montgomery, *Daniel*, 404; quoted in Walvoord, 302.
31. Wiersbe, 145.
32. Ibid., 152.
33. Ibid., 153.

Chapter Fourteen

34. Leon Wood, *A Commentary on Daniel* (Grand Rapids: Zondervan, 1973) 278-79, quoted in Walvoord, 328.

35. Stephen Miller, editor, *Daniel* (Nashville: Broadman and Holman, 1998), 78.
36. Wiersbe, 161.
37. Ibid., 162-164.
38. Miller, 81-83.

Chapter Fifteen

39. Walvoord, 345.
40. Ibid., 379.
41. Ibid., 353.

Chapter Sixteen

42. Walvoord, 353.
43. S.P. Tregelles, *Remarks on the Prophetic Visions in the Book of Daniel,* 7th *ed.* (London: Sovereign Grace, 1965), 162. This is also the reading adopted by translators of the *New American Standard Bible*, quoted in Walvoord, 371.
44. Wiersbe, 176.
45. Ibid., 178.

CONTACT INFORMATION

To order additional copies of this book, please visit
www.redemption-press.com.
Also available on Amazon.com and BarnesandNoble.com
Or by calling toll free 1-844-2REDEEM.

CPSIA information can be obtained at www.ICGtesting.com
Printed in the USA
LVOW07s0320221115

463623LV00003B/5/P